THE HOCKEY COACH'S MANUAL

A Guide to Drills, Skills, Tactics and Conditioning

Michael A. Smith

FIREFLY BOOKS

Cataloguing-in-Publication Data

Smith, Michael A.
   The hockey coach's manual

ISBN 1-55209-183-X

1. Hockey – Coaching.   2. Hockey – Training.
I. Title.

GV848.25.S64   1997   796.962'077   C97 930879 8

A FIREFLY BOOK

Published by
   Firefly Books Ltd.
   3680 Victoria Park Avenue
   Willowdale, Ontario
   Canada M2H 3K1

Published in the U.S. by
   Firefly Books (U.S.) Inc.
   P.O. Box 1338, Ellicott Station
   Buffalo, New York 14205

Produced by
   Bookmakers Press Inc.
   12 Pine Street
   Kingston, Ontario K7K 1W1

Design by
   Roberta Voteary

Printed and bound in Canada by
   Friesens
   Altona, Manitoba

Printed on acid-free paper

Front cover photograph
© Ron Chapple/Masterfile

Legend

RD	Right Defenseman		direction)
LD	Left Defenseman		Player movement (arrow shows direction)
RW	Right Wing		
LW	Left Wing	....	Shot (arrow shows direction)
C	Center	⟶	Full Stop
X₁	Right Defenseman	-------	Pylon
X₂	Left Defenseman		Point of contact
X₃	Right Wing	I	
X₄	Left Wing	△	
X₅	Center	— · —	
	Pass (arrow shows		

CONTENTS

Chapter Three:

Chapter Four:

COACH'S MANUAL

INTRODUCTION

NORTH AMERICAN HOCKEY HAS HISTORICALLY BEEN A GAME LEARNED ON NATURAL ICE. PICKUP games played on a frozen pond or river or on a family backyard rink attracted players of all ages who honed their skills during endless winter days.

The pond system provided something besides basic hockey skills, however. It bred a toughness into players that has characterized the Canadian game. Younger players who were banged around, knocked down or checked into the snowbank by more experienced players quickly learned not to show hurt or humiliation. Though often at a disadvantage in size, skill or ability, these younger players chose instead to get back into the play, driven by a competitive urge to win against their older rivals.

Today, organized hockey has largely taken the place of yesterday's improvised backyard games. Most of what young players once learned on the pond is taught within the more structured program of a community club. Guiding that transition from friendly to formal competition is the coach, who must provide leadership and instruction for the team.

To fulfill his role as a teacher, today's coach must apply new, improved methods of training to develop his team's skills and elevate its level of play. Players arrive at their first practice as unrelated individuals of differing athletic abilities and skill levels. It is the coach's job to transform these players into a team. Matching a tactical strategy to suit the team's strengths (or weaknesses) calls for the coach to lay out a season-long training schedule timed to bring his players to their optimal level of conditioning and skill within the playing season.

Hockey is not a complex game. Yet it is only through careful planning and organization that the coach can distill the game's principles into a simple and understandable method. This book provides such an introduction to several of the important elements of coaching. It will help the coach build a team by utilizing both dryland and on-ice training, designed to develop athletic abilities and fundamental hockey skills. Individual chapters on defensive and offensive strategies, which span the range from conservative to aggressive styles of play, will help the beginning coach make a tactical plan to suit his team. This book provides a blueprint methodology for many of the elements of coaching. Coaches should use it but not be limited by it. I encourage each coach to creatively augment this formula with his own drills, plays, systems and tactics.

A team sport, hockey is often referred to as a feeder game, similar to basketball, lacrosse and soccer. Outstanding individual skills are important, but it is the display of teamwork during the execution of hockey tactics that allows winning clubs to excel. Hockey is an intense, physical game of skill, in which success is tied to a sound underlying framework. In this sense, it resembles jazz. Both jazz and hockey demand basic skills. Each also demands improvisation from individual players who can contribute something extra. Individuals play off each other and constantly adjust to one another. In hockey, just as in jazz, too much planning can ruin everything. Similarly, team success depends on coaching leadership that fosters athletic discipline and shapes winning team strategies without inhibiting the spirit of competition and the freewheeling enthusiasm that has characterized generations of backyard games.

SKILLS, TACTICS & CONDITIONING

"And we taught our children to be honest and truthful. That it didn't pay in the long run not to be truthful. That usually it was caught up with and it went against them."

Etta Hartley
Foxfire 3

HOCKEY IS A GAME THAT NEEDS GOOD SOUND FUNDAMENTAL SKILLS, SKILLS THAT BECOME THE foundation for both the individual players and the team. Team tactics, for example, cannot be executed without the proper level of skill development. It is essential that coaches learn what skills should be stressed for their team. The fundamental skills must be taught at a pace that permits the individual players to execute them correctly. The desired high-tempo execution of the skills that is sought by and expected of elite teams cannot be attained without proper development of these skills.

A key ingredient to successful coaching is to know what your team is able to do and how to build upon it. While the content of practices should vary for different age groups, there is often a tendency to include drills in a team's practice that are beyond the players' abilities. Coaches need to know what is appropriate.

Teaching team tactics must take a logical path. First, certain tactics are often too complex and difficult for young or poorly skilled teams to execute. Second, some of these tactics must be broken down and taught in parts in order for players to learn them. Introducing tactical skills in this manner allows the complete system to be put together gradually. (The total should be greater than the sum of the parts.) Third, there should be common ground between the players and the tactical system. The players' abilities must fit the system, and the system must complement their abilities.

It is important for the coach to have an understanding of the physiological guidelines of skill development. The physical development determines the level of conditioning for each age group. The players need to have reached the necessary developmental levels prior to the introduction of certain conditioning techniques. What may be good for a team of 15- or 16-year-olds may not be good for other age groups.

AGE BREAKDOWN: This chapter uses three age groups, with each subdivided into two more groups. The young group is 11 and under, the middle group is 12 to 15 years of age, and the older group is 16 and over. The determining factor in these group distinctions is physical development. The young group is prepuberty, the middle group is going through and just completing puberty, and the older group is approaching physical maturity.

The book uses the following age breakdown:

Young Group:	9 and under	10 and 11
Middle Group:	12 and 13	14 and 15
Older Group:	16 and 17	18 and over

The young age group's training is quite basic. All the skills, such as skating, passing, shooting and buckhandling, should be introduced by the age of 11. These drills, however, should be taught patiently with simple and direct drills. With regard to tactics, this age group should become familiar with the rink areas—slot area, deep zones, blue-line area and along the boards. "Rink sense" reflects a knowledge of the different areas. Even these young players should learn why the areas are important, how the areas contribute to the game, and they should be developing a feel for their responsibilities when they are positioned in them. The conditioning has to be simple. Off-ice drills should include easy running, acrobatics and basic coordination drills. On-ice conditioning drills should cover only the normal skill-development drills.

The middle age group's training is more intricate. The skills should be taught by combining two

r more skills when possible. A shooting drill that also utilizes passing and skating, for

xample, can be implemented. Three aspects of tactical training can be taught to the

iddle group. First, it is time for the players to learn and apply certain concepts to their

ame, such as the difference between offense and defense, attack and counterattack, the

mportance of being a man-down or a man-up, controlling the slot area and playing the

an. Second, they are also ready to learn individual tactics, such as backchecking, a one-

an forecheck, a two-man forecheck and man-to-man coverage. Third, it is time to

ntroduce noncomplex team tactics. This age group should demonstrate a growth of

hockey sense," which is a general knowledge and understanding of the game. The

onditioning process remains uncomplicated, and off-ice training can feature aerobic runs

nd general strength development through calisthenics and gymnastics. Coaches should

arefully monitor any type of weight training. On-ice conditioning should combine easy

hort-duration drills along with the general skill-development drills.

The older group's training should be comprehensive. While constantly reteaching the

asic skills, coaches should stress the execution of the skills at a high tempo. The individual

actics should be sound. The older group's proficiency with individual tactics should permit

he team to learn and execute more complex systems. Off-ice conditioning should

ntroduce strength training using weights. A strong aerobic base should be developed. On-

ce conditioning should emphasize a sound anaerobic base, with special attention paid to

peed and quickness.

Skills

KEY POINTS

Table 1 lists the degree of concentration for skating, shooting and puck skills.

1. Skill improvement enables the coach to make use of drills that are more advanced in difficulty and tempo.

2. Failure to master the proper skill technique prevents any execution at a high tempo.

3. Do not introduce complex skills to the younger group.

4. The middle group should begin to show a degree of mastering the fundamental skills.

5. The older group, for the most part, should be able to execute most skills at a high or near-high tempo.

Table 1. Skills

Skills	Young Group		Middle Group		Older Group	
	9/under	10-11	12-13	14-15	16-17	18/over
Skating						
Forward	XX	XX	XX	XXX	XXX	XXX
Backward	X	XX	XX	XX	XXX	XXX
Turns	X	XX	XX	XX	XXX	XXX
Spins	X	X	X	XX	XXX	XXX
Jumps		X	XX	XX	XX	XXX
Stops	X	XX	XX	XXX	XXX	XXX
Tumbles and Falls		X	X	XX	XXX	XXX
Sprints		X	XX	XXX	XXX	XXX
Puck Skills						
Dribbling	X	XX	XX	XXX	XXX	XXX
Puck Control	X	XX	XX	XXX	XXX	XXX
Sweep Pass	X	XX	XXX	XXX	XXX	XXX
Snap Pass			X	XX	XXX	XXX
Backhand Pass		X	X	XX	XXX	XXX
Drop and Back Pass		X	X	XX	XX	XXX
One-Touch Pass			X	XX	XX	XXX
Pokecheck		X	X	XX	XXX	XXX
Feet to Stick		X	XX	XX	XXX	XXX
Shooting						
Sweep	X	XX	XX	XXX	XXX	XXX
Snap			X	XX	XXX	XXX
Slap			X	XX	XXX	XXX
Backhand	X	X	XX	XX	XXX	XXX
Rebounds	X	X	XX	XX	XXX	XXX
Tip-Ins/Deflections	X	X	XX	XX	XXX	XXX

The symbol X indicates the suggested age level at which the skill should be introduced. The puck skill "dribbling," for example, should be included in the practices of the youngest group—9 and under. The puck skill "snap pass" should begin with the 12-to-13-year-old group. Wrist and forearm strength is not usually developed until this age. Insufficient strength prevents proper execution of the skill.

The symbol XX indicates the age level at which significant improvement in the execution of the skill should be seen. The skill "backhand shot," for example, while introduced to the 9-and-under group, should improve with the 12-to-13-year-old group.

The symbol XXX indicates the age level at which the skill should be used proficiently. This means the skill should be executed at a high or near-high tempo. This is totally dependent on the skills being properly taught and learned at an early age.

Skill Drills

KEY POINTS

There should be a progression of skill drills from the stage of introduction to high-tempo execution. In general, coaches should advance their players to the more complex drills only after the basic drill—Drill 1, in this example—is executed at a high level of proficiency. Drills 1, 2 and 3 provide an example of progression in both difficulty and pace.

1. Drill 1 can be used by all age groups. The tempo or speed of execution should increase with the age groups.

2. Drill 2 can be used by the middle and older age groups and should increase in tempo with age.

3. Drill 3, if executed at a high tempo, can be used by the older groups and possibly advanced middle groups.

Puckhandling and Turns.

Purpose: To introduce turns while handling the puck.

Description: Performed by skating along the two blue lines and the red lines. Obstacles are used as guides.

Tempo: Drill is executed from slow to half speed.

Participation: The entire team with one player following right after another.

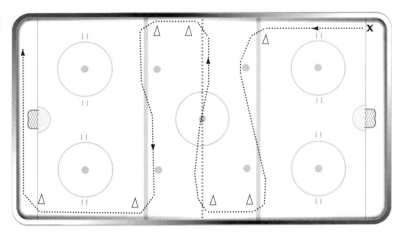

Drill 1 is a simple one that has the players carry a puck around the rink, with pylons for direction. The drill provides plenty of room to maneuver. The turns are neither difficult nor sharp. The speed of the drill is moderate, which gives the players time to concentrate on handling the puck. This is a good drill to introduce the puck skill dribbling to any age group.

Puckhandling and Circles. 2

Purpose: To emphasize handling the puck while executing crossovers.

Description: Players skate around each of the five face-off circles. This enables the players to practice crossovers to the left and right while handling the puck.

Tempo: Drill is executed from half to full speed.

Participation: Team is divided into groups of three to five players. The second group starts when the first group has completed its crossovers at the second face-off circle.

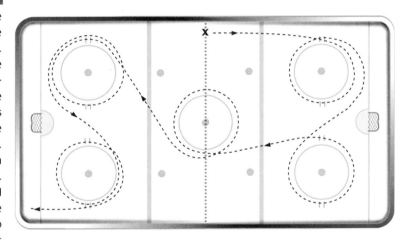

Drill 2 is more difficult. It combines crossover skating with puckhandling. The players skate around each face-off circle while stickhandling with the puck. The speed of the drill ranges from moderate to high tempo. Crossovers and dribbling need to be developed if this drill is to be executed properly. The coach must control the speed to ensure proper execution of the skills. Introduce the drill by having the player skate crossovers while stickhandling without the puck. Good for middle age groups that have shown improvement in the two skills.

Puckhandling and Stops. 3

Purpose: To emphasize puckhandling at a high tempo.

Description: Players skate the length of the ice executing turns and stops at the blue and red lines. Use pylons as guides.

Tempo: Executed at full speed.

Participation: The team is divided into groups of three. The second group leaves after the first group passes the near blue line.

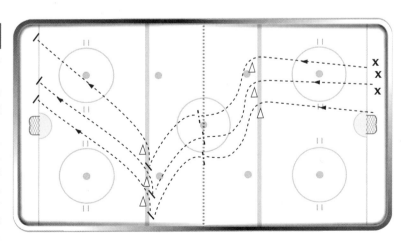

Drill 3 combines the skills of skating forward, stops and puckhandling. To be effective, the drill should be executed at full speed. Players need to make strong stops and quick starts and handle the puck while skating fast and showing good technique. Poor technique will force the players to lose the puck or to do the drill at a slower speed. For older age groups.

Individual Tactics

KEY POINTS

Table 2 lists the individual tactics. There are two kinds of tactics: individual and team. Players must learn individual tactics prior to team tactics. Success at team tactics depends on the development of individual skills and individual tactics. The fore-checking situation of 1-on-1 is an individual tactic. The 1-2-2 is a team tactic. The 1-on-1 forechecking situation is utilized, however, in the 1-2-2. Thus, it is critical that the players be able to execute the 1-on-1 situation if the 1-2-2 system is to be effective.

1. Most individual tactics should be introduced by 10 to 11 years of age.

2. Most tactics are not executed at a high tempo until 16 to 17 years of age.

3. Generally, individual tactics coincide with the development of skills and with increasing understanding of the game.

Table 2. Individual Tactics

	Young Group		Middle Group		Older Group	
	9/under	10-11	12-13	14-15	16-17	18/over
Skills						
Forecheck						
1-on-1	X	X	XX	XXX	XXX	XXX
1st Man/2nd Man		X	X	XX	XXX	XXX
5-Man			X	XX	XXX	XXX
Backcheck						
Man-to-Man	X	X	XX	XXX	XXX	XXX
Open Man			X	XX	XXX	XXX
Team Coverage		X	X	XX	XXX	XXX
Breakouts						
Positional	X	X	XX	XXX	XXX	XXX
One-Man Passes		X	XX	XXX	XXX	XXX
5-Man		X	XX	XX	XXX	XXX
Move to Open Space		X	X	XX	XXX	XXX
Screening			X	XX	XXX	XXX

The symbol X indicates the suggested age level at which to begin teaching the tactic.

The symbol XX indicates the age level at which significant improvement should be made in executing the tactic.

The symbol XXX indicates the age level at which the tactic should be executed at a high tempo.

Tactical Drills

KEY POINTS

There should be a progression of individual tactical drills from introduction to high-tempo execution. Forechecking drills 1, 2 and 3 provide examples for such a pattern.

1. Drill 1 is a basic individual forechecking drill. It is an excellent drill to teach 1-on-1 forechecking. It can be used by all age groups, including the youngest.

2. Drill 2 is an excellent introductory one for 2-on-1 forechecking. It can be used by the middle and older groups and possibly by the 10-to-11-year-olds.

3. Drill 3 teaches the more advanced 2-on-1 forecheck. It can be used by the older groups and the middle groups if they have mastered the individual tactics taught in Drills 1 and 2.

Forechecking.
Purpose: To teach the forwards to check the puck carrier (1-on-1).
Description: An offensive player (O1) carries the puck behind the goal line. The checking forward skates parallel to O1, staying a half-stride behind while maintaining the same speed. X1 forces O1 to go behind the net, prevents him from cutting up the middle and is in a position to skate O1 into the boards and to maintain physical control.
Participation: Two players. Can be executed at both ends.

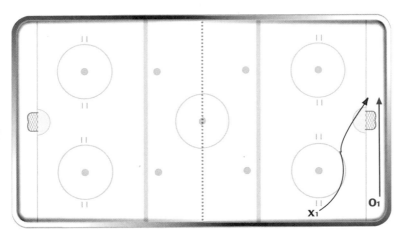

Drill 1 simply teaches the player to forecheck the puck carrier in a 1-on-1 situation. This drill enables the player to utilize both the boards and the net for assistance. The speed of the drill is slow to high tempo, with the younger groups using the slower speeds. The drill teaches how to play the man and not allow the puck carrier to get around or to cut behind the checker.

Forechecking.
Purpose: To teach two forwards to pressure the puck carrier 2-on-1.
Description: The puck carrier (O1) starts a few feet ahead of the first forechecker (X1). X1 forces O1 to the boards. The second forechecker (X2) moves in from a different direction. The first forechecker should play the man, and the second takes the puck.
Participation: Three players. Can be executed at both ends.

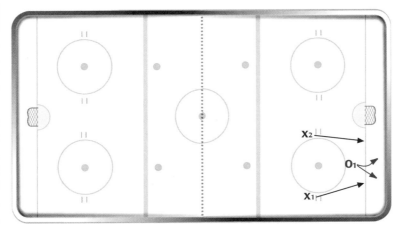

Drill 2 is a more difficult one. It teaches forechecking the puck carrier in a 2-on-1 situation. It calls for the two checkers (X1 and X2) to work in tandem. It is important for the players to work together; otherwise, the puck carrier (O1) will be able either to carry the puck or to pass it. The speed of this drill is moderate to high tempo. What is learned in Drill 1 about 1-on-1 forechecking is essential for this drill to be useful.

Forechecking.
Purpose: To teach the Center and puck-side wing to forecheck in tandem in the neutral zone.
Description: An offensive player (O1) moves up the ice with the puck. The Center (X2) pressures O1 toward the puck-side wing (X1), who can then double-team the puck carrier. X1 and X2 can also practice interchanging, with the Center going to the boards and the wing pressuring O1.
Participation: Three players.

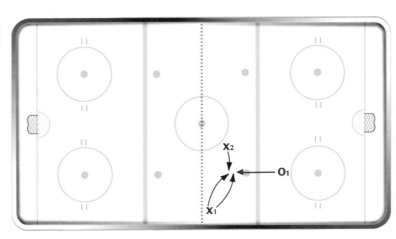

Drill 3 is a high-tempo game-situation drill. It teaches 2-on-1 forechecking in the neutral zone. The two forecheckers (X1 and X2) must check the puck carrier (O1) in the open ice. They do not have the net or the boards to assist them. What is learned in Drills 1 and 2 is essential for this drill.

21

Team Tactics

KEY POINTS

Table 3 lists the developmental progress for team tactics that coaches can expect from their players. There is more on the execution of specific team tactics in Chapter Three (Defensive Strategies) and Chapter Four (Offensive Strategies). Table 3 indicates that the conservative systems are normally introduced to the 10-to-11 and 12-to-13-year-old groups. Puck-control systems, which generally combine conservative and aggressive elements, are introduced primarily at the 12-to-13-year-old level, when most players develop sufficient skills to utilize such systems. Puck-control systems are not emphasized until players reach the 14-to-15-year-old group, when they are able to handle this type of system. Aggressive systems, on the other hand, are not introduced until the 14-to-15-year-old group. The older groups should be able to execute nearly all the systems at the high-tempo level.

1. Systems and tactics are totally dependent on the skill levels of the individual players.

2. Team tactics are, for the most part, taught only in a limited sense to the younger groups. The youngest group, 9 and under, for example, is not normally developed enough to warrant use of hockey systems.

Table 3. Team Tactics

Tactic	Young Group 9/under	10-11	Middle Group 12-13	14-15	Older Group 16-17	18/over
Forechecking						
1	X	X	XX	XXX	XXX	XXX
2			X	XX	XXX	XXX
3				X	XX	XXX
Breakouts						
1	X	X	XX	XXX	XXX	XXX
2			X	XX	XXX	XXX
3				X	XX	XXX
Center Ice						
1			X	XXX	XXX	XXX
2			X	XX	XXX	XXX
3				X	XX	XXX
Offensive Zone						
1		X	XX	XXX	XXX	XXX
2			X	XX	XXX	XXX
3				X	XX	XXX
Defensive Coverage						
1		X	XX	XXX	XXX	XXX
2			X	XX	XXX	XXX
3				X	XX	XXX
Power Play						
1		X	XX	XXX	XXX	XXX
2			X	XX	XXX	XXX
3			X	XX	XXX	XXX
Penalty Killing						
1		X	XX	XXX	XXX	XXX
2			X	XX	XXX	XXX
3				X	XXX	XXX
Face-Offs	X	X	XX	XX	XXX	XXX

The symbol X indicates the suggested age level at which to begin teaching the tactic.

The symbol XX indicates the age level at which significant improvement should be made in executing the tactic.

The symbol XXX indicates the age level at which the tactic should be executed at a high tempo.

Key:
1 indicates simple basic systems.

2 indicates systems that combine basic with some innovation.

3 indicates aggressive and advanced systems.

Conditioning

KEY POINTS

Table 4 lists the breakdown of the components of conditioning by age. There is more on specific conditioning drills in Chapter Five (Tactical Dryland Practice). This table simply indicates the recommended age level at which coaches should begin or continue training for the specific components of conditioning.

1. The age group 10 to 11 has had a little more than half of the components introduced, while the 9-and-under group has had only five.

2. By age 12 to 13, all skill components have been introduced.

3. The table illustrates that conditioning does not become a major part of a hockey program until the middle age groups. Even then, it is not until the older groups that conditioning receives due emphasis.

Table 4. Conditioning

	Young Group		Middle Group		Older Group	
	9/under	10-11	12-13	14-15	16-17	18/over
Motor Skills						
Balance	X	X	X	X	X	X
Agility	X	X	X	X	X	X
Coordination	X	X	X	X	X	X
Speed of Movement	X	X	X	X	X	X
Speed of Reaction		X	X	X	X	X
Power			X	X	X	X
Physical Fitness						
Flexibility	X	X	X	X	X	X
Muscular Endurance			X	X	X	X
Muscular Strength						
Body Weight		X	X	X	X	X
Weight Training			*X	X	X	X
Aerobic			**X	X	X	X
Anaerobic				X	X	X

The symbol X indicates the age level at which conditioning should begin.

* Weight training for this group needs to be monitored carefully.

** Used only in a limited sense.

SKILL DEVELOPMENT

"Skill is the knowledge and ability to quickly and properly execute the fundamentals. Being able to do them is not enough. They must be done quickly. And being able to do them quickly isn't enough either. They must be done quickly and precisely at the right time."

John Wooden
Former UCLA Basketball Coach

HOCKEY SKILLS ARE THE ESSENTIAL TOOLS FOR THE GAME. THOSE PLAYERS WHO master the game's skills become top-level players. When all other things are equal—speed, quickness, strength, conditioning, toughness—the player with the skills will win out. There no age too young to begin developing the skills, nor is there an age to stop skill development. onstant practice perfects and maintains a player's skills. Baseball players take batting practice, olfers and tennis players take lessons and spend hours on the court, while pass receivers and uarterbacks work daily on pass plays. Hockey players also must continue to work on their skills.

Coaches need to stress the fundamentals. No one is ever too good to practice the fundamental kills. Just the opposite is true—one is good because he has developed the skills and works to maintain them.

Dryland training provides the opportunity for both the coach and the player to work on skills when ice is not available. Each skill can be improved through dryland training. Every player, ndividually or as part of a group, can work on skills by himself.

This chapter provides a number of exercises to develop skills. They are broken down into wo general groups: athletic ability and hockey skills. Each category lists a few dryland drills, xercises or training techniques, many of which are the same as or similar to those used on ice. Dryland training contains no revolutionary aspects or secrets. It simply employs what has been arried out for years on ice.

Every sport can be analyzed in terms of its required essential athletic abilities. Each sport has its own specific physical demands that help make it unique. Yet each sport also shares physical demands with other sports. The athletic abilities, which are basic motor skills essential to hockey, include balance, agility, coordination, speed of movement, speed of reactions and power. Young players can be trained in these abilities through a solid general physical-education program. Coaches, however, should not rely on this alone. Focused training for hockey's required essential athletic abilities should become part of your coaching program. Improvement in the various athletic abilities will enhance the development of the hockey skills.

The individual hockey skills—skating, puckhandling (which includes passing and stickhandling), shooting, bodychecking and goaltending—are broken down into categories listed at the opening of each section. Hockey skills are complex. Proper execution may appear to be simple, but learning the skill is not.

Balance

Balance is the ability to maintain one's center of gravity and equilibrium.

There are two types of balance:
1) static balance—maintaining the center of gravity and equilibrium in a stationary position.
2) dynamic balance—maintaining the center of gravity and equilibrium during movement.

Static Balance. Balance on one foot with the other foot at a right angle to the first leg. This exercise can be varied by having the athlete shut his eyes, paddle a ping-pong ball or bounce a tennis ball off the wall.

1

2 Balance on a board with a cylinder underneath it. This exercise can be varied by having the athlete shut his eyes, paddle a ping-pong ball or bounce a tennis ball off the wall.

Balance on one foot with the other foot extended to the rear. This exercise can be varied by having the athlete shut his eyes, paddle a ping-pong ball or bounce a tennis ball off the wall.

3

4 Balance on one knee with no other part of the body touching the floor. This exercise can be varied by having the athlete shut his eyes, paddle a ping-pong ball or bounce a tennis ball off the wall.

Dynamic Balance. Walk across a fence or a narrow balance beam.

5

Walk on a straight line. A variation is to hop on one leg along the straight line.

6

Agility

Agility is the ability to change direction and body position while moving. Agility is important to the development of the hockey player's mobility and shiftiness. It is essential in all aspects of the game. Hockey is a game of movement as well as physical contact, and the greater one's agility, the better his level of skill performance will be.

The suggested method of doing the agility exercises is to perform them in a series. For example, do one-legged hops for 30 yards and repeat 3 times; 5 forward rolls and repeat 3 times; 5 spins in 30 yards and repeat 3 times.

1 One- and two-legged hops. Player executes these in different directions: forward, backward and sideways.

2 Leapfrog. Two or more players are needed. The drill should be executed quickly.

3 Forward and backward rolls. It is important that the player ends up on his feet after the last roll.

4 Spins and sharp turns. During this drill, the player should visualize himself as a football running back.

5 Football log rolls, jumps and hopscotch. These drills combine a series of different jumps.

6 Duckwalk. For the player to perform it properly, this drill requires a strong sense of balance.

7 Crab walk. In this drill, players should practice first moving forward and then moving backward.

8 Wheelbarrows. Two players are required for this drill. Players should practice both forward and backward movement.

Coordination

Coordination is the ability to perform body movement in a smooth and fluid manner. Coordination calls for correct interaction of the various parts of the body. There are different types of coordination: hand-to-hand, hand-to-eye, eye-to-foot and hand-to-foot.

A goaltender needs excellent eye-to-hand and eye-to-foot coordination. Other players should also work on eye-to-foot and eye-to-hand coordination, which simulates eye-to-stick coordination. In a broad sense, coordination is the culmination of the other athletic abilities in action.

1 Run in pairs:
1) tossing a tennis ball back and forth or 2) kicking a soccer ball back and forth. A more advanced exercise is to do both simultaneously.

2 Play catch with two to five balls in small groups of two to six players.

Catch a football **3** on the run.

Use yo-yos in both hands. **4**

5 Two people play catch with a tennis ball while each uses a yo-yo in one hand.

Speed of Movement

Speed of movement is the ability to move either the body or parts of the body through space. The actual speed is the rate of the movement. Speed of movement is important in hockey because of the nature of the game.

Hockey is a game of motion—the players with the higher rate of speed enjoy certain benefits that improve their level of performance.

Shuttle Runs. Run specified **1** short sprints (10, 15 or 20 yards) repeatedly. The best method is to do shuttle runs for a specified time (30, 45 or 60 seconds). A player's speed improves as the number of repetitions in the time period increases. (An increase from 12 to 14 repetitions shows an increase in speed of movement.)

Run short distances, **2** such as 50 yards, from a moving start. By running with a 15-yard start, the reaction time (normally measured from the start on a whistle) is eliminated. The 15 yards also allows the athlete to be at top speed by the time he reaches the beginning of the 50 yards.

3 Play ping-pong.

Speed of Reaction

Speed of reaction is the time or interval between the presentation of a stimulus and the first sign of a response. An example of how to understand speed of reaction is to line up three athletes and have them run at the sound of the whistle. Most likely, they will get off the whistle at different intervals. The first to move would have the quickest reactions, while the third would have the slowest.

Speed of reaction is important in hockey because of the high number of stimuli—the puck, the opposition, the blue lines, the boards and the referees, to mention a few. The statement "the players must react to the different situations that arise during a game" summarizes the need to work on speed of reaction.

Have one player **1** drop a ruler between the thumb and index finger of another. Have the player close his hand when the ruler is dropped. This permits the coach to gauge the player's speed of reaction and improvement according to the number of inches the ruler drops.

2 With arms extended, hold your hand with a coin or washer in the clenched fist. Drop the object and catch it again before it hits the ground.

Have one player **3** throw a ball to another whose back is turned toward him. Have the thrower call after he has released the ball. The catcher can turn on the call and catch the ball. This exercise combines auditory and visual response. As the players improve on catching the ball, make the distance shorter between thrower and catcher.

4 Have players practice moving off the mark at the sound of a whistle.

5 Have one player swing a stick at both ankle and shoulder levels. The other player jumps over the stick when it is at ankle level and ducks under the stick when it is at shoulder level.

Power

Power is the ability to move either your body or an object rapidly through space. Power is important for a hockey player for many reasons. First, the power that is exerted during the stride contributes to the speed of movement and balance in skating. Second, power in the arms contributes to both the speed of the release and the velocity of a shot.

Third, power is important for the parts of the game that call for a combination of mobility and physical strength: plays in the corners, in front of the net and along the boards. To improve power, the athlete must combine speed and strength. Power can also be defined as the product of velocity (or speed) and force (or strength).

1 **Vertical Jumps.** Performed in three different fashions: 1) a standing vertical jump in which the athlete makes one jump concentrating on obtaining maximum height; 2) vertical jumps repeated for a specified time period using the same height (for instance, jump on and off a bench, chair or table, etc.); 3) a series of vertical jumps over objects of varying height while moving forward. A weight belt or vest can be worn to increase the development of power.

Standing Broad Jumps. **2**
From a standing position, the athlete leaps forward for maximum distance.

3 **Semi- or Half-Squats.** Carrying a barbell across his shoulders, the athlete performs half-squats by squatting until the knee forms a 90-degree angle. Place a chair or bench behind the athlete to provide a restricting barrier. Do the exercise for either a specified time period or a specified number of repetitions.

Straddle Run. **4**
An exaggerated run that puts all the weight on one leg at a time. The run can also be performed with weights held in the hands or with a weight belt or vest.

Arm Push-Ups. **5**
The athlete assumes a push-up position. Instead of doing actual push-ups, the athlete thrusts himself off the floor in a manner similar to push-ups and claps his hands. It is most effective to repeat the exercise for a specified time period.

Skating

SKILLS

Skating is the foremost basic skill in hockey. If you cannot skate, you cannot play the game. Whether you are a recreational or an elite player, the better you skate, the more enjoyment you will experience from the game. Most of the athletic abilities discussed earlier are ingredients of the skating skill. Balance, coordination, agility, power, speed and fitness constitute, in combination, the art of skating. Work on these will improve the player's athletic ability needed for skating. To prevent player laxness, coaches should stress the proper skating stance during all the skill development. The proper stance: the player's head is aligned directly over his feet to maintain his center of gravity; the knees are bent so that the player looks as if he is about to sit in a chair; and the head should be up and moving left and right to develop peripheral vision. The skating drills can be done either with or without hockey sticks.

Forward

Backward

Turns

Spins

Jumps

Tumbles and Falls

Stops

Dekes

Forward. **1** Exaggerated straddle run. This drill emphasizes the actual skating stride. Push off with one leg as you do on skates.

2 Straddle run with weights. When the player wears a weight belt or vest or carries hand weights, the straddle run develops leg power.

Practice both **3** Drills 1 and 2 carrying another player on your back.

Straddle jump **4** along a bench. The player straddles a bench while moving along it. Stress placing all the weight on each leg alternately. This drill also develops leg power, particularly when weights are used.

Backward. **5** Hip movement. To work on hip movement, run backward, keeping both feet as close to the ground as possible. Swing the hips in a backward swivel motion to simulate the hip movement on ice.

6 Leg movement. Run backward, bringing each leg directly behind the body. This is another method of skating backward.

Shoulders to the front. Work this **7** drill in pairs. One player moves forward, attempting to get by the second player, who is moving backward. The player moving backward must keep both shoulders in front of the other player. It may help to set up ropes as guides so that players do not go too wide. When a defenseman plays a man 1-on-1, it is critical that both shoulders stay in front of the opposing man.

8 **Turns.**
Lateral stepove[r]
This drill is similar to the
on-ice method. The play[er]
moves laterally, head a[nd]
shoulders to the front. T[he]
outside leg (right leg wh[en]
moving left) is brought [up]
and over the inside leg.
The player pushes off
simultaneously with the
inside leg.

Forward
crossovers. **9**
Place pylons to guide
the turn. The body
must lean into the turn.
When the player moves
to the left, for example,
the outside leg, or left
leg, goes high and wide
while the inside leg
goes short and straight.

10 Backward
crossovers. Place
pylons to guide the turn. The
body must lean into the turn.
When the player moves left,
the outside leg, or right leg,
goes high and wide while
the inside leg goes short
and straight.

11 **Spins.**
While
running, make a series
of 180-degree spins
(half-spins).

While
running, **12**
make a series of 360-
degree spins.

13 Have a line
of players
follow the leader, who
makes a series of 180-
and 360-degree spins
while running at
varying speeds.

Jumps. **14** Do a series of jumps over objects of different heights. These jumps should be done forward, backward and sideways. To be safe, start with low heights and increase according to ability.

15 Use a single bench, and have the player do a series of different jumps:
1) sideways,
2) forward,
3) backward and
4) forward and backward.

16 Leapfrog, skip rope, one-legged hops and two-legged hops.

Tumbles and Falls.
A forward roll can be done **17** in two ways, and both should be practiced: 1) drop a shoulder to make it a shoulder roll, or 2) place both hands on the ground, and bring the body directly over by tucking the head underneath.

Backward **18** rolls. A backward roll is done by lying on your back and bringing your legs up and over your head while shifting the body weight from your back to your feet.

19 Football log rolls. This is a football drill that has at least three players lying prone and performing full-body rolls simultaneously. This drill includes changing direction and alternating positions.

Knee drops. **20** The player practices dropping to one knee and getting back to his feet. Then he practices dropping to both knees and getting back to his feet.

21 Belly flops. The player simply falls on his stomach and regains his feet.

22 Backward falls. The player runs backward and falls on his rear end. To regain his feet, the player rolls to his side and gets up. The player should practice rolling to both sides.

23 **Stops.** Two-legged stops. Run at an easy pace, and simulate stopping with both legs. Once the player has done this properly, practice stopping and starting: stop and then start just as one would do on ice.

Do these drills practicing proper foot placement and body position.

One-leg stop. Run at an easy pace, and simulate stopping on one leg. Once this has been turned, practice stopping on one leg and starting just as one does on the ice. **24**

Practice dekes by running at pylons or other stationary objects, such as trees or chairs, and practice the following moves:

Dekes. Head **25** dekes. The player looks one way and moves in the other direction.

26 Shoulder dekes. The player drops one shoulder as if to move in that direction but actually moves in the other.

Stop and spin. **27** The player will stop in front of the pylon, spin 360 degrees and move past the object. When used on ice, this drill either commits the opposition into moving up to the player, who then moves by him, or makes him completely stop, permitting the player who has not stopped his momentum to get by.

28 Acceleration. The player practices accelerating past the object by changing the length of his stride and by increasing or decreasing his speed.

Puckhandling

SKILLS

This category includes the aspects of hockey in which a player handles the puck, with the exception of shooting and goaltending. Some players have a better knack for puckhandling than do others. For them, it is more natural, but everyone can improve through practice. The earlier the player begins to concentrate on this skill, the better he will be at it as he grows older. Coordination (hand-to-feet, eye-to-hand and eye-to-feet), strength (especially in the forearms), speed of hand movement and speed of reaction are directly related to puck-handling skills. Body position is critical: head up, shoulders level, back straight; and players should use a narrow hand grip of 10 to 14 inches. Floor pucks are excellent on wooden and concrete floors, the preferred surfaces. Tennis balls and rubber-coated baseballs work well on dirt and grass fields. Otherwise, use floor pucks or tennis balls, as specified in individual drills.

Dribbling

Puck Control

Passing (Receiving and Attempts)

Dekes

Pokechecking

Face-Offs

Feet-to-Stick Puckhandling

Dribbling.
1 Stationary stickhandling. The player simply stands still and moves the floor puck or tennis ball. The key to quick dribbling is to keep the stick as close to the puck as possible when dribbling. Construct a wooden box that will limit the height the stick moves above the puck. This will enable the player to be conscious of how high he raises the stick. As the player improves, use boxes that are not as high. Use only floor pucks.

2 Move while stickhandling. The player moves forward, backward and to both sides while dribbling. Both floor pucks and tennis balls can be used.

3 Stickhandling obstacles. Place pylons, and stickhandle between them. This drill should be done while moving.

4 Stickhandle with light weights. To develop strength in the forearms, take a bladeless stick and a weight. By placing the end of the stick in the hole of the weight, the player can stickhandle the weight. Begin with a low weight, and progress upward.

5 Stickhandle with wood. To increase quickness, take a small piece of wood (approximately 2 inches square) and drill a hole in the center. Place the end of a bladeless hockey stick in the hole, and dribble the wood. (Drills 4 and 5 should be done together. Drill 4 is for strength, and Drill 5 is for quickness.)

6 **Puck Control.** Spins. Practice spins of 180 degrees and 360 degrees while dribbling with either a floor puck or a tennis ball.

7 Balance. The player balances either a tennis ball or a floor puck on a hockey stick while running at an easy pace. During the run, do spins, turns and stops. Both hands should be on the stick.

8 Stickdribble. The player dribbles either a tennis ball or a floor puck on the blade of the stick. The drill can be done in both a stationary and a moving position. This drill teaches the "touch" of the puck.

9 **Passing.** Two players pass a floor puck or tennis ball back and forth, practicing the sweep, flip, snap, lift, backhand, backpass and drop pass.

Many of the drills for on-ice practice can be duplicated for dryland sessions.

Three to five players form a **10** circle and pass one or more floor pucks among themselves. This drill can also be executed with a person in the middle to intercept the passes. Dryland training should place some emphasis on developing puck control when receiving a pass.

11 The player ha[s] a second person roll tennis balls toward him. The player works on taking the pas[s] without the tennis balls bouncing off his stick. I[f] player can control the tennis ball, the puck should be easy, since it does not have the boun[ce] of a tennis ball.

Practice Drill **12** 11 with the player moving forward taking passes from a number of players. When this drill is done with floor pucks, have the player pass to the next person he reaches in the line.

For young players age 5 to 9, it may be wise simply to practice the bio-mechanics of passing. Have the players go through the proper motion of passing. Gradually move to light, then regular pucks. For many young players, a regular puck is too heavy at the beginning, which prevents the development of the correct passing technique.

The player should practice drills similar to the dekes in the earlier skating category. There are some additional drills as well.

13 **Dekes.** Have two players stand 3 to 5 feet apart. One player has a floor puck and moves at the second player practicing head and shoulder dekes and spins.

14 The player stands stationary with a floor puck and practices dekes as if he were coming out of a corner and an opposing defenseman is coming to meet him.

Pokechecking. **15** The player moves backward with his stick in one hand. The stick is moved sideways as he moves backward. A second player can move toward him, with the first player attempting to pokecheck the puck. Ropes should be put up to keep the second player from going too wide.

16 **Face-Offs.** The player works on the "draw" by practicing stick movements on imaginary opponents. The player should work on taking draws to his forehand and his backhand. He can also practice body position and body movement off a face-off.

17A Practice actual face-offs between players using tennis balls or floor pucks. A number of situations can be practiced during these face-offs:

To the backhand

17B To the forehand

17C Toward the net

17D To a wing breaking behind the opposing center

17E To specific spots, such as a point man or a wing

17F Gain body control over the opposing center: 1) screen the center from moving by you, and 2) use your body to force the center off the puck.

These face-offs can become competitive by keeping score for face-offs won and lost.

Feet-to-Stick Stickhandling. **18** The player stands stationary, and a second player passes either tennis balls or floor pucks at the player's feet. He redirects the passes to his stick.

19 The player remains stationary while dribbling the floor puck or tennis ball back and forth between his feet and stick. The player should work at getting both feet equally adroit at this.

20 The player runs at an easy pace while another player makes passes to his feet. The first player redirects the passes from his feet to his stick.

Shooting

SKILLS

Shooting is a prominent part of North American-style hockey. The "big shooters" are well known and emulated by the younger players. Many of the top *scorers*, however, do not possess blistering shots.

Recent research on shooting suggests that the quickness of the shot release is more important than its velocity. Some believe that a good goaltender can stop nearly any shot if he is permitted to get set. If this is the case, the key is to release the shot before the goalie gets set. The release then becomes a critical aspect of shooting and deserves special attention.

Players with the higher percentages of blocked and deflected shots are usually pausing: they possibly don't know where the net is, have lost control of the puck, are "winding up" or "cocking the wrists" or are undecided about whether to shoot.

Dryland shooting drills practice different aspects of shooting other than velocity and accuracy. These two aspects are important, but the other aspects, such as screening, rebounds, tip-ins and deflections, are important to shooting and scoring. Remember that there is no such thing as a "garbage goal"—a goal is a goal is a goal. The list of drills that follows should be used for all shot types.

Sweep

Snap

Slap

Backhand

Flip

Rebounds

Tip-Ins

Deflections

Dekes

Screening

1 **...earm Strength**. ...evelop strength in the forearms, take a ...eight or a partially filled ...ch bottle and tie it with ...rope to a hockey stick. Extend both arms, and ...se the weighted object ...y rolling the stick in the ...ands. As the strength in ...orearms increases, add weight to the object.

2 **Wrist Strength**. Do this drill during the course of a day's activities—while watching TV, reading, riding in a car—and do it frequently. Carry a rubber ball around with you, and periodically squeeze it. Work on both wrists, and do the drill for a specified number of repetitions: squeeze 10 times, rest 60 seconds, squeeze 10 times, and so on.

3 **Shot Velocity.** Practice shooting with a weighted puck: 1) drive short nails into a rubber puck; 2) drill holes into a regular puck, and fill them with solder; or 3) make a puck out of heavy material, such as iron or steel.

4 **Shot Quickness**. Practice shooting with lighter pucks, such as a floor puck. To make a light puck, simply drill holes in a regular puck.

5 **Snap Shot**. Shoot tennis balls to develop the snap shot. Tennis balls are most conducive to this type of shot. Simply snap the wrists. Gradually move from tennis balls to floor pucks, then to regular pucks.

6 **Backhand Shot**. Players should spend considerable time practicing the backhand. Dryland training on this shot saves the coach time during on-ice sessions.

7 **Body Positions.** ...ave the players practice shooting from ...odd body positions: on ...ne knee, on two knees, ...the wrong foot, on the stomach. During the ...ourse of a game, many ...opportunities arise that require a shot from an ...odd position, and these should be practiced ahead of time.

8 **Net Awareness.** Have a second player either roll tennis balls or pass floor pucks to a first player, who shoots on a net (or an area marked off as a net) without looking toward the net. This drill teaches the shooter to be conscious of his location in relation to the net and to shoot without first looking.

9 **Rapid Shooting**. Have the players shoot a number of tennis balls or floor pucks in a specified time period, such as 10 pucks in 10 seconds. Keep score by having targets worth 5 points, "on-net" shots worth 1 point and "off-net" shots worth either 0 or minus 5 points.

Two things can be done to make the dryland shooting drills realistic. First, make an object out of plywood or heavy cardboard to simulate a goalie; the legs can be wide for goalie pads. Second, a stuffed duffel bag can be placed between the shooter and the goal area (either stationary or swinging on a rope) to simulate a defenseman.

10

Rebounds.
One player
shoots either tennis balls or
floor pucks at a shooting board
or a wall, and the second player
shoots the rebound.

Two players and several
tennis balls are used in this **11**
drill. One player stands 5 to 20 feet from
a wall and throws the tennis balls one at
a time so that they come off the wall in
the air to the second player, who is
responsible for the rebound. This drill
simulates the circumstances when a shot
comes off the goaltender in the air and a
player has to bat at the puck in the air.

12 This drill
requires three
players: a shooter, a
rebounder and a
defenseman. The
rebounder has to fight
with the defenseman to
get the rebound from
the shooter's shots.

Tip-Ins and Deflections. **13** This drill requires two players. One player shoots floor pucks along the floor, and the second player deflects or tips the shots.

14 This drill requires two players. One player shoots floor pucks off the ground—6 inches to 2 feet—and the second player tips the shots in the air.

15 This drill requires two people, and a third person can be used as a defender. The first player lifts a shot high in the air, and the second player knocks the shot down with a glove and shoots on the net. If a third person is used, have him play the body of the second player.

16 Three players are required for this drill. The first player shoots wide of a defender, and a second player deflects the shot on net.

A few comments on the different types of shots may be useful for guidance:

Slapshot

Nearly every player practices the slap shot too much. There is no question that the slap shot is a potent scoring weapon, but the number of opportunities to use it effectively are few compared with the other types of shots.

Snapshot

The snap shot has, in recent years, grown in its use and effectiveness. It is the quickest shot in terms of release—the wrists snap—and should be used within 30 feet of the net.

Backhand Shot

The backhand shot has fallen into some degree of disuse, particularly with the advent of the curved stick.

17 **Dekes.** The player practices passing off after faking either a sweep or a slap shot. The player actually goes through the initial motion of shooting but passes off prior to releasing the shot.

18 The player practices passing off after faking either a sweep or a slap shot. The player actually goes through the initial motion of shooting but passes off prior to releasing the shot.

19 **Screens.** This drill requires two players. One player shoots, and the second player screens the goal area for the shooter. This drill teaches one player how to shoot with a screen and the other player how to actually screen for a shooter. The screening player should learn to place himself directly between the goaltender and the shooter.

Bodychecking

The North American style of hockey emphasizes giving and receiving bodychecks. Every aspect of the game is influenced by physical contact. It is extremely important that proper checking techniques be taught. Many players check as if throwing a block for football— arms up and elbows out. The coach must accept the responsibility for teaching his players how to check properly. For the player giving a check, agility, balance and strength are important. For the player who is taking a check, agility, balance and strength determine whether he can remain in the play. Toughness and courage are essential for the physical aspect of hockey, and these qualities are acquired, not taught. Proper training techniques and drills, however, will contribute to a young player's development of these prerequisites for bodychecking.

Shoulder

Hip

Full Body

Board Play

Forward

Backward

Legal Interference

Man-to-Man (Shadowing)

Shot Blocking

A technique for teaching bodychecking uses American football dummies. (Stuffed duffel bags can also be used.) The dummies are hung on a wire and can be swung back and forth to simulate moving players. The dummies are used to train players to take physical contact as well.

1 Checks.
Have the player perform the technique at a slow speed. As his technique improves, have the player increase the tempo of the checks. Once the player has acquired the techniques of the various checks, have him perform a series of checks on different dummies.

2 Skating.
erform figure-8s, crossovers, quick stops, backward and forward spins, knee drops, belly flops and glides within e area of the dummies. his drill emphasizes the eed to keep one's head up. Use pucks for puck control and stickhandling.

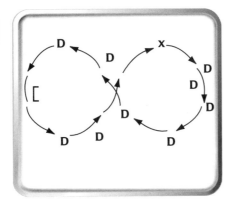

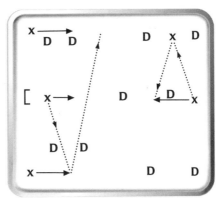

3 Passing.
Perform a series of two-man give-and-go's, two-man, three-man and five-man rushes and two-man and three-man passing drills through the tackling dummies. This drill emphasizes the attempt and reception of passes while being hit by the opposition.

4 Shooting.
Perform a series with one man receiving and shooting the puck, shooting from a specific pot and moving toward he net at various angles o shoot. This drill again teaches the ability to shoot while under the hreat of being checked. also teaches the player to get the shot off without the opponent ocking the shot (replace puck with volleyball).

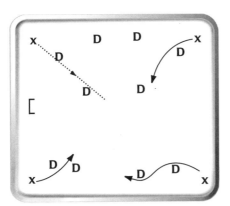

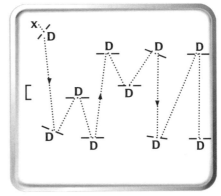

5 Bodychecking.
Have each player move to each dummy, performing the different types of checks—body, shoulder, hip and stick. Begin with the dummies stationary, and as the players improve, begin to swing the dummies.

6 Break the players into two to four teams of three to five players each. One net is used to limit the play to a confined area. Use a volleyball or something similar. Each team tries to score but also tries to prevent the other from scoring into the one net. Two rules should be used: 1) only two steps can be taken with the ball, and 2) only two steps can be taken prior to checking.

Have the players form two lines: one line is of checkers; the other line, offensive players. The offensive player runs between a wall and the defensive player. Players can perform these drills with sticks. The defensive player practices:

Board Play. Taking the offensive player into the boards while running forward.

Taking the offensive player into the boards while running backward.

Angling the offensive player out of the play by forcing him into the wall.

Legal Interference.

Moving interference. Teach this technique using three players: A, B and C. Player B is the puck carrier, Player A is a checker chasing B, and Player C is a teammate of B and moves between B and A to hinder Player A's attempt to check Player B. The interference by Player C takes Player A out of the play momentarily, permitting Player B to make a play with his check eliminated.

Lacrosse and basketball make good use of both picks and interference. The hockey coach can learn much from watching these sports and talking to coaches of these sports. The use of moving interference enables one player to force another player out of the play without actually making contact. The use of picks enables one player to screen another player out of the play. Both moving interference and picks should be taught to players at an early age.

9 Picks.

Teach this technique using three players: A, B and C. Player B is the puck carrier, Player A is a checker, and he is moving toward an area that will permit him to check Player B. Player C is a teammate of Player B and, knowing the intentions of Player A, moves to the same area. Player C will place himself between Players B and A, permitting B to remain unchecked and stopping Player A's intentions of checking Player B.

Man-to-Man (Shadowing). **10**

Players form two lines. One will be offensive, the other defensive. The offensive player moves downfield, and the defensive player runs alongside, shadowing him. Stress: 1) the defensive player keeps the offensive player away from the play by staying between him and the play, and 2) the defensive player practices "split vision" by constantly switching his sight from his check to the actual play. The offensive player will attempt to cut inside. The defensive player can prevent this by keeping his body parallel to the offensive player at all times.

11 Shot Blocking.

This drill requires two players: a shooter and a defensive player. The shooter takes easy shots in the direction of the defensive player. The defensive player practices blocking shots on one knee, on both knees and on his side. This drill teaches the player who will block shots to get his timing right. Stress the development of good timing and anticipation. These two aspects, plus courage, make a player a good shot blocker.

Goaltending

Many coaches consider the goaltender to be the most important position in hockey. Coaches look to a strong goaltender to secure a team's defense. A paradox is evident, however, when one views the training of the North American goaltender, who is often virtually ignored in practice. The coach may run a practice for the team, and the goalie is used only for drills. Even valuable shooting drills become sessions where the players unrealistically blast away at the goalie. If the goaltender is so critical to the success of a team, why is he ignored in practice? Some coaches believe that only former goaltenders can coach goalies. That idea is a myth. Goaltenders need certain abilities and skills, and the coach should help develop these. Coaches who understand the goalie's needs can effectively train him. This section presents a number of dryland drills that can develop the skills of a goaltender.

Stance

Movement

Skating

Agility

Falls

Catching and Stick Gloves

Puck Control

Freezing

Stickhandling

Clearing

Equipment needed for dryland goaltending training: some type of a hockey goal (a wooden one will suffice), tennis balls, floor pucks, regular pucks, rope, goalie pads, goalie gloves, goalie stick, weights (5-to-25-pound weights), yo-yos, medicine balls, volleyballs and chairs. All the goaltending drills on dryland should be done with the goalie in his appropriate stance whenever possible.

1 Stance. The goalie does a forward roll and comes up in the stance. The coach can toss a tennis ball back and forth with the goalie to increase the difficulty of the drill.

2 The goalie does a backward roll and comes up in the stance. The coach can toss a tennis ball back and forth with the goalie to increase the difficulty of the drill.

3 Have the goalies work in pairs, with one goalie on the back of the other. The goalie on the ground practices maintaining his stance while walking around with his partner on his back. The coach can toss a tennis ball back and forth with the goalie to increase the difficulty of the drill.

4 The goalie does a duck-walk, with his upper body (from the waist up) straight, keeping the proper stance and position of his hands. The coach can toss a tennis ball back and forth with the goalie to increase the difficulty of the drill..

5 The goalie does a series of jumps (one- and two-legged) and half-squats. The goalie maintains his stance as he finishes each move. The coach can toss a tennis ball back and forth with the goalie to increase the difficulty of the drill.

6 Have the goalies pair up and move about together, tossing a tennis ball back and forth while moving around in the stance.

The goalie should do the next three drills with gloves and stick. The coach can toss tennis balls at the goalie in the following drills to make them more difficult.

7 Movement/Skating The goalie practices moving to both sides by sliding the front leg and dragging the back leg.

8 The goalie practices coming out of the net and moving back to it. This drill also teaches awareness of the goal and the goal area.

9 The goalie practices his mobility around the net by moving around the net in both a forward and a backward manner.

Agility.
The goalie does **10** a series of forward rolls.

11 The goalie does a series of backward rolls.

The goalie does a series of rolls **12** combining both forward and backward rolls.

13 Have the goalies pair up and play tag in a confined area. The tag game should be played with the goalies in different positions: on one knee, on both knees, while duckwalking and in a regular stance.

Have the goalie jump over low **14** objects (hockey sticks will suffice). The jumps should be done on one leg or on both legs in forward, backward and sideways directions. (The coach can toss tennis balls at the goalie in these drills to make them more difficult.)

Falls.
The goalie practices falling on his stomach. To make this drill more difficult, have the goalie dive at the blade of a stick held by the coach. As the goalie dives, the coach pulls the stick away. Doing these in a series forces the goalie to get quickly to his feet and dive again.

The goalie practices falling on his back and on his side. To make this drill more difficult, tie a tennis ball on a string and hang it from the crossbar of the net. With the tennis ball swinging back and forth, the goalie, as he falls, reaches for the ball to simulate stopping a puck that has gotten behind him.

The goalie practices dropping to one knee and returning to his regular stance. He then does the same by dropping to both knees. It is recommended that the goalie wears either his goalie pads or basketball knee pads to protect his knees.

Catching and Stick Gloves. **18**

The goalie stands 3 to 10 feet away from a wall, with a second person a short distance behind him. The second person tosses tennis balls off the wall, and the goalie practices catching the ball in his glove hand or blocking the ball with his stick or blocking glove.

The goalie **19** stands in the net, and a second person hits tennis balls at the goalie with a tennis racquet. The balls should be directed at specific spots and not necessarily with high velocity. The drill is to train proper technique. Blasting shots tends to hinder the teaching idea.

20 In a similar manner to Drill 19, have the goalie make saves from different positions: on his knees, on his stomach and on his side. Do not hit the tennis balls with high velocity. This drill is to familiarize the goaltender with making saves from unusual body positions.

The goalie **21** has a yo-yo on his stick hand and plays catch with a second person using only his catching hand. This drill teaches eye-to-hand coordination.

22 Have a group of two to six goalies volley with one to three volleyballs while kneeling. To make this drill more difficult, have the goalies simultaneously toss a tennis ball around the group. This group should contain at least four.

Blocking. The goalie stands in the net, and a second person **23** hits tennis balls at his body with a tennis racquet. The balls are directed at specific spots for the goalie to make leg saves, chest saves, and so on. Do not hit the tennis balls with high velocity.

24 The goalie drops to both knees and stops the tennis balls with his chest. Be sure the goalie is able to cover up after the save. He should not permit the tennis ball to become a rebound.

The goalie lies on his **25** side and stops tennis balls with the upper leg.

Puck Control (Clearing, Stickhandling and Freezing). 26 Wearing both goalie gloves, the goalie stickhandles floor pucks with his goalie stick.

27 The goalie practices going behind the net and stopping tennis balls to simulate stopping regular pucks behind the nets. Tennis balls should be used, since floor pucks do not maintain the velocity that a regular puck does on ice.

The goalie stands in the net, and a second person hits **28** tennis balls at him with a tennis racquet. The balls are randomly directed at the goalie, who freezes every shot.

Wearing both gloves, the goalie practices shooting floor **30** pucks with his goalie stick. The goalie should work on lifting the pucks, since this is often necessary when attempting to clear the puck out of the zone.

29 The goalie practices protecting a floor puck from a second person. The goalie uses only his stick to ward off the tennis racquet that the second person uses to get at the ball.

DEFENSIVE STRATEGIES

"Defense is dull, boring, commonplace. It is the unimaginative plodding attention to duty. It is grit and determination. There is never a day you can't use defense. All you need is the decision to put out. To give 100 percent.

What defense discloses is character.... So defense is a matter of pride."

Dr. George Sheehan
Running and Being

HOW A TEAM PLAYS WHEN THE OPPOSITION HAS CONTROL of the puck is defensive play. As unglamorous as it is to fans and players alike, good defense often determines the winning team in a close contest. All successful teams play defense well, because even on defense, there is always the opportunity to grab the tempo away from the opposition and move onto the offensive.

Two things are important, therefore, when a team plays defense: how it defends against the opposition and how it regains control of the puck. The two elements are closely linked.

The defensive strategy is the team's overall style of defensive play. There are three basic styles: (1) conservative, (2) positional with elements of aggressive play and (3) aggressive. For each distinct strategy, a number of systems fit for each of the three zones—forechecking, neutral zone and defensive zone.

Defensive strategies are important for the coach and team. Each coach must be comfortable with the style of play and specific systems that his team uses. This is one area in which good sound coaching pays off. Defensive play requires hard work and discipline.

Conservative

KEY POINTS

The conservative strategy of defensive play is simple and basic. It is a good strategy to teach young teams, but there are times when all teams can utilize a conservative strategy. Systems that are conservative serve the purpose of introducing players to important defensive concepts that will stay with the players as long as they play hockey.

1. The objectives are simple and direct.

2. Most conservative systems are positionally balanced, with no one position being the key.

3. Serves as a good starting point or introduction for team defense.

4. Discipline from the players is important.

FORECHECKING

The 1-2-2 forechecking system is a conservative one. Its purpose is to defend the opposition through strict positional play. It attempts to control the boards but also has the five players positionally balanced in the offensive zone.

Basic Alignment. The Center (C) forechecks the puck carrier; the wings (LW and RW) stay wide, checking the opposition's wings; and the defensemen (LD and RD) play inside the wings.

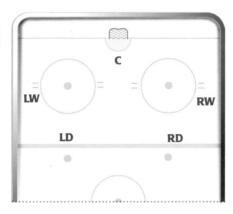

1

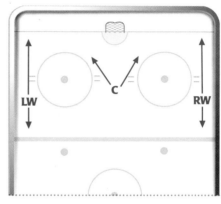

2 The objective is to force the opposition to move the puck to areas checked by the LW and RW. The Center prevents the opposition from moving up the middle.

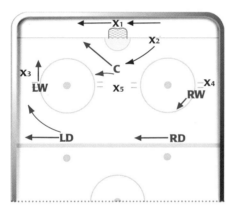

3 An example: The Center checks X1, the LW has the option of either moving in if the Center has X1 in check or staying with X3. The RW moves back and is responsible for X4. The LD moves toward the boards and can pinch along the boards. The RD is responsible for the deep middle.

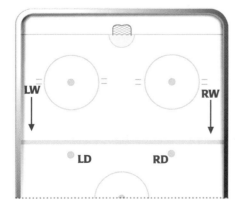

4 If the opposition beats the forecheck, one or both wings are in a position to fall back. This prevents any 3-on-2 breaks by the offense.

NEUTRAL ZONE

The 1-2-2 system of neutral-zone play is similar to the forechecking 1-2-2. It is forechecking in the neutral zone. Neutral-zone play needs to be similar to the forechecking.

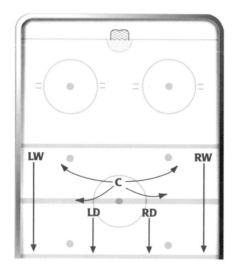

1 **Basic Alignment.** The wings keep the opposition's wings in check to prevent them from cutting to the middle. The Center forechecks the puck, with emphasis on forcing the play to the outside. The defensemen play toward the middle and stand up in the neutral zone.

The objective is **2** to force the opposition either to turn the puck over in the neutral zone or to dump the puck in. If the puck is dumped in, the wings interfere with their checks, one defenseman picks up the opposing center (X5), and the second defenseman retrieves the puck.

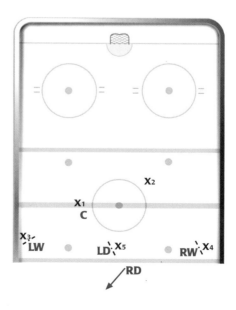

DEFENSIVE ZONE

How a team defends in its own zone is important. A team's mistakes in its own end mean good scoring opportunities for the opposition. To succeed, it is important that defensive-zone play is taught clearly by the coach and understood well by the players. The "zone defense" is conservative. The roles for the players are clear—stay in your zone, and control that area.

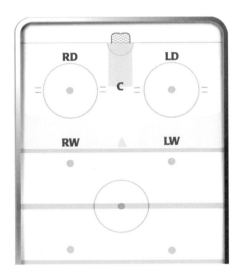

1 **Basic Alignment.** The defensive zone is divided into five zones. There is some overlapping of the zones. The wings cover the two points, the Center covers the slot area, and the defensemen cover from the front of the net to the corners.

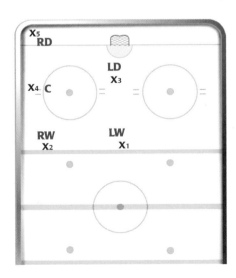

2 The objective is to defend the opposition by covering the entire defensive zone. In a normal situation, one defensive player should be able to play the man or the puck in his zone. For example, if the opposition has the puck in the corner, the puckside defenseman (RD) will play him. The other defenseman (LD) is in front of the net. The Center covers from the slot to the boards. The wings cover their respective points, maintaining a position between the puck and the point.

Positional With Element of Aggressiveness

KEY POINTS

This type of defensive strategy lets the defensive team have at least one aggressive player. While most of the players remain in positional roles, the aggressive player is permitted to be aggressive or attack the opposition. This puts additional pressure on the offensive team.

1. It combines conservative positional play with aggressiveness.

2. It encourages pressuring the puck carrier with two players.

3. It introduces innovation into team defense.

FORECHECKING

The 1-1-3 forechecking system combines aggressiveness with conservative positional play. One forward, usually a wing, plays back in a defensive role. This prevents any 3-on-2 breaks. The other two forwards assume aggressive forechecking responsibility. They exert pressure on the puck.

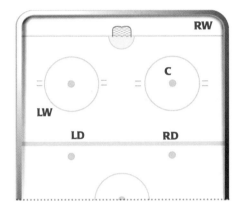

1 **Basic Alignment.**
Two forwards, the Center and puck-side wing (RW), have forechecking responsibilities. The off-side wing (LW) stays high in the offensive zone. The LW is in a position to move back in a defensive role or to move to the slot area. The defensemen take normal positions.

The objective is to have the off-side wing (LW) shut down **2** the far board, which forces the opposition to bring the puck up through the forechecking forwards (C and RW). The first forward (RW) forechecks the puck carrier, and the Center is in a position to assist the RW or move to the puck if the RW is beaten. The RD is permitted to pinch in, and the LD is responsible for the middle.

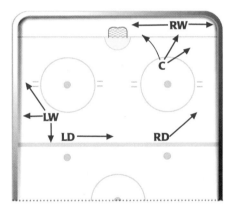

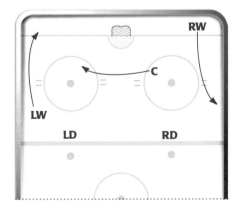

3 The forwards often have to rotate. As the play moves from one side to the other, the off-side wing (LW) becomes the forechecker and the puck-side wing (RW) assumes the defensive forward's role. The Center's role remains constant.

NEUTRAL ZONE

The 1-1-3 system of neutral-zone play is similar to the forechecking 1-1-3. It is an extension of the forechecking system.

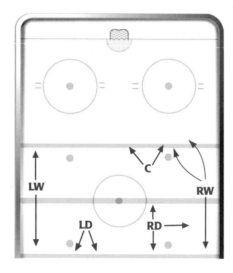

1 Basic Alignment.
The off-side wing (LW) plays conservatively, closing down the outside lane. One player, either the Center or the puck-side wing (RW), forechecks the puck aggressively. The second forward has the option of attacking the puck or dropping back. If it is the puck-side wing, he covers his wing. If it is the Center, he covers the middle. The off-side defenseman (LD) plays conservatively. The puck-side defenseman (RD) reacts to the second forward. If the second forward attacks, the defenseman moves wide toward the boards. If the second forward stays back, the defenseman moves to the middle (if it is the wing who drops back) or to the boards (if it is the Center).

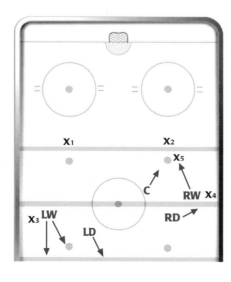

2 The objective is to pressure the puck carrier with two forwards (RW and C) while the puck-side defenseman (RD) attacks the puck. The conservative play of the off-side wing (LW) and the defenseman (LD) allows the forecheckers to pressure the play in the neutral zone.

DEFENSIVE ZONE

This defensive strategy is one step beyond the "zone defense." The defensive zone is divided into five zones, which permits the players to adapt when one zone or its player is outmanned or flooded. Success depends on the players working as a unit. The players need to understand why and when they can leave their zone.

Basic Alignment. Each player has a zone for which he is responsible (see Diagram 1, page 71). In addition to the zone, each player is responsible for one opponent. The wings cover the opposition's defensemen, the Center covers the opposition's center, and the defensemen covers the opposition's wings. The man-to-man coverage encourages more overlapping of the zones than in the strict "zone defense."

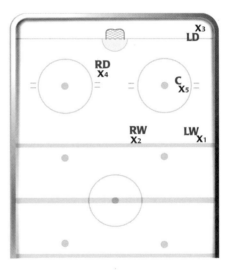

2 The objective is to prevent the opposition from creating 2-on-1, 3-on-1 or 3-on-2 situations. When the opposition overloads one zone, a defensive player leaves his zone to cover his check. When this happens, the other players increase their zone areas. For example, if the Center goes to the corner to help the LD and to cover his check, the Center's zone (slot area) is vacated. The RW and LW become responsible for the high slot, and the RD for the deep slot.

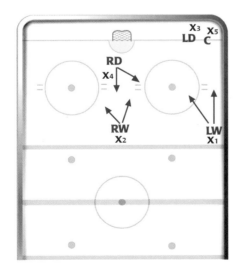

Aggressive

KEY POINTS

The aggressive strategy of defensive play attempts to take the initiative away from the offensive team. This is done by placing intense pressure on the puck. Such pressure forces quick passes (often to players in check), which can be difficult to execute properly. The aggressive systems are not for young or inexperienced teams.

1. It attempts to take the initiative away from the offensive team.

2. It stresses putting pressure on the puck and forcing the puck carrier to pass.

3. It encourages systems that are free-flowing with constant motion, with emphasis placed on attacking the opposition at all times in all areas.

4. It should be used only with older and experienced teams.

FORECHECKING

The 2-1-2 forechecking system is an aggressive one. Its objective is to pressure the puck at all times in the offensive zone in an attempt to force a turnover. This system demands hard work and determination, since the players are in constant motion.

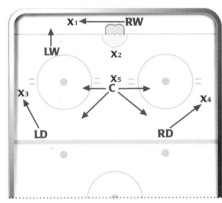

1 **Basic Alignment.** Two forwards (either the wings or the first two forwards) attack the puck. The third forward (usually the Center) plays in the high slot. The two defensemen play wide on the blue line.

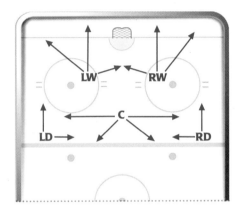

2 The objective is to keep constant pressure on the opposition. The two forecheckers (LW and RW) are aggressive at all times. The third forward (C) backs up the two forecheckers and can become a backchecker or cover for either defenseman, who may pinch along the boards to cover the opposition's wings or the puck. The third forward also is responsible for the middle of the ice and must keep the opposition's center in check.

3 The aggressiveness of the forecheckers usually causes the players to interchange positions. For example, when the puck carrier has been pressured and forced to move the puck, the realignment will likely have the Center on the blue line, the LD in along the boards and the two wings in deep.

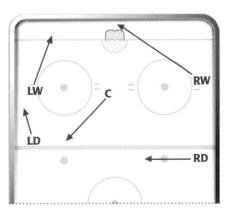

NEUTRAL ZONE

The 2-1-2 system of neutral-zone play is similar to the 2-1-2 forechecking system. It calls for constant pressure from two forwards, usually the wings.

Basic Alignment. **1** The two wings play up and pressure the puck. The defensemen play wide and are responsible for the outside lanes. The Center is responsible for the middle. The Center's role is to assist the wings and to back up either defenseman should he pinch or move to the boards.

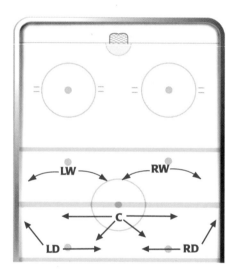

2 The objective is to keep constant pressure on the puck. If the puck is forced up the middle, the Center is in position to move in. If the puck is forced to the boards, a defenseman moves in and the Center backs him up. The constant movement encourages the three forwards to interchange with each other. There should always be one forward moving in the direction of the middle to allow the defensemen to be aggressive.

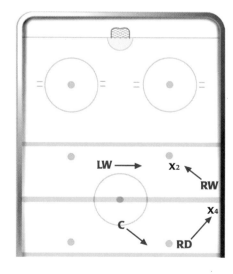

DEFENSIVE ZONE

A 2-1-2 alignment in the defensive zone is an aggressive system. The strategy is to pressure the offensive team with two players. The defensive unit does not want to allow the offense the time to set up or to control the play. It is the Center who is the key player, and it is he who is the second attacker.

1 **Basic Alignment.** The two defensemen are deep, one in the corner on the puck and one in front of the net. The wings are on the point, and the Center plays the slot area.

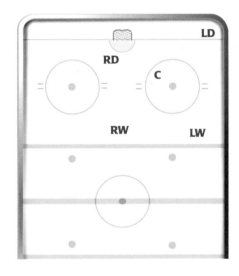

2 The Center is the key player. His positioning permits him to move to help any of the other four players. This means that two players can attack the puck.

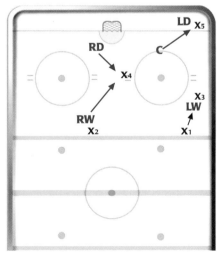

3 If X5 has the puck in the corner, the LD immediately plays him. The Center moves to help the LD. The LW checks X3 to prevent a pass to him. Either the RD or the RW checks X4, depending on his positioning. The points are open, but the aggressive strategy risks this to attack the puck. This strategy allows the wings to check their points if the puck ends up there.

79

OFFENSIVE STRATEGIES

"We believe that team play requires not only kindheartedness and desire to help one's partner but also a high level of individual skills, a creative approach and initiative."

Anatoli Tarasov
The Road to Olympus

CHAPTER FOUR

TEAM PLAY IS ESSENTIAL IN HOCKEY, AND THERE IS NO greater showcase for quality team play than on offense. Coordinated offensive strategies are essential to create the attack. General principles that utilize all hockey skills guide the offense from its defensive-zone breakout to its attack on the opposition's net.

This chapter presents three styles of offensive strategies for team play—positional play, puck-control play and aggressive attacking—and details how each of them is executed in the different zones—breakouts, neutral-zone or offensive-zone attacks.

It is important that a coach choose a style of play according to the philosophy for his team and the strengths and weaknesses of its members. Young, inexperienced teams will likely benefit from the discipline of positional-play systems, while older and more physical teams who have already mastered positional play can further elevate their game and dominate their opponents with aggressive play.

Positional Play

KEY POINTS

Positional play is, for the most part, conservative. All teams must have a knowledge of positional play, and all teams must utilize positional play sometime during a game. This style of play is the foundation for the other offensive styles. Players and teams must always have a positional basis for their play on the ice. Positional play requires the basic skills. It is a useful style of play, and it does not require an advanced level of skill development.

1. It introduces a basic knowledge of offensive team play.

2. It is the basic starting point for all types of offensive play.

3. It teaches positional discipline.

4. It teaches total ice awareness.

5. It teaches interrelationships of positions.

6. It teaches individual positional responsibility.

BREAKOUTS

The "balanced breakouts" have the forwards play their basic positions. The wings are along the boards, the Center is in the middle, and the defensemen are in their normal areas around the net. This style of play permits the team to use all five positions. No one position is emphasized. The outlet passes are normally short and quick.

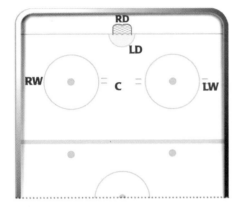

1 **Basic Alignment.**
The wings (LW and RW) are on the boards, the Center is in the middle, and one defenseman (RD) is behind the net while the other (LD) is in front of the net.

The normal options **2** for this breakout have the RD pass to the LW, RW or Center. It is important for the forwards to get to their positions. The wings need to come back to the hash marks, and the Center deep to the slot. The RD, knowing the positions, can make a short pass to any of the forwards.

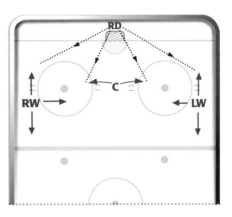

When the opposition shuts down **3** the normal outlet pass routes, the offensive unit must react to it. One possible option has the LD move from the net area toward the left corner. He may or may not swing through the right corner. The LD becomes a fourth possible player for an outlet pass. Normally, the wing (LW) will move across the face-off circle. This gives the RD two players (LW and LD) to pass to on his left.

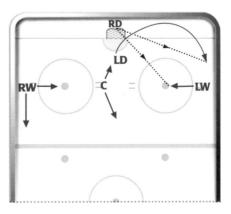

NEUTRAL ZONE

The "balanced attack" in the neutral zone is similar to the "balanced breakouts." The wings are on the boards, the Center is in the middle, and the defensemen are in their normal positions. This style of play permits the offensive unit to move in the direction of any three forwards.

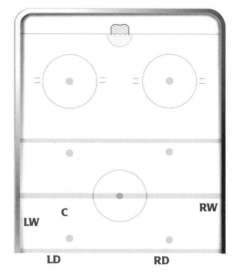

1 **Basic Alignment**
The wings are on the boards, the Center is in the middle, and the defensemen are in their normal position near the blue line.

2 The typical play has a defenseman (LD) make a short pass to either the LW or the Center.

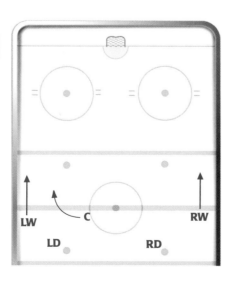

3 A variation has the Center swing across the middle to receive a pass. The wings stay along the boards.

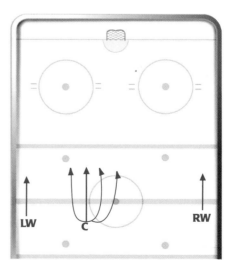

4 The three forwards usually move up the ice in a fairly straight line. The purpose is to stay in their normal positions, which the others know and which places them to receive a pass.

The two wings stay on the boards and break for the net. The Center enters the zone in the middle and moves to the slot.

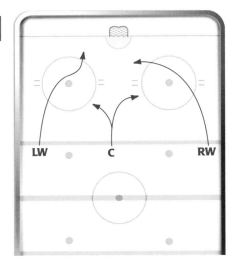

OFFENSIVE ZONE

The positional play in the offensive zone is simple. The forwards go to the net. One forward thinks defensively to assure that there are no 3-on-2 counterattacks. The forwards enter the zone "balanced."

A second option is for one wing (LW) and the Center to break for the net. The second wing (RW) moves to the slot.

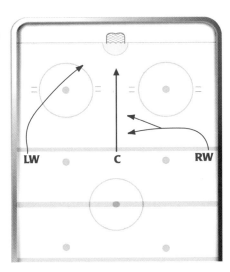

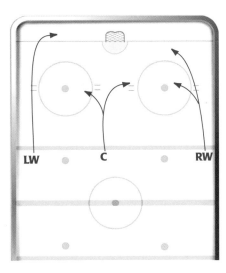

One wing (LW) stays along the boards and goes deep. Either the second wing (RW) or the Center, usually the one who enters the zone last, stays in the slot, and the other can go deep or to the net.

The defensemen are normally conservative and stay on the blue line. They are allowed to move to the high slot when the opportunity arises. When one defenseman (LD) moves in, the second defenseman (RD) moves back a few feet to cover.

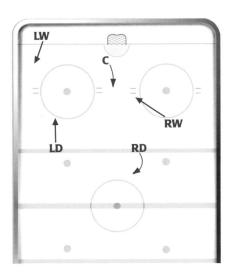

Puck-Control Play

KEY POINTS

Puck-control play is an advanced stage of positional play. It combines discipline with innovation. The purpose of this style of play is to maintain control of the puck. This is done with sound passing. Normally, the players move within a defined area, which permits them to move the puck confidently when a man becomes open. This style of play is dependent on the skill of passing. Skating and puckhandling are also important.

1. It combines discipline and innovation.

2. It requires more than adequate use of the passing, puckhandling and skating skills.

3. It teaches anticipation.

4. It teaches movement to open areas.

5. The interchanging of positions is important.

6. Team patience is needed to make use of the puck control.

BREAKOUTS

The "puck-control" breakout stresses maintaining control of the puck. This is done with a combination of good positional play and sound execution of the skills. It is important for the puck carrier to have a second outlet to pass to and to control the puck rather than always trying to move forward.

Basic Alignment. The forwards are in the normal areas—wings on the boards and the Center in the middle. The defensemen are both behind the goal, one on each side of the net. This permits the defensemen to pass the puck between themselves. The defensemen normally maintain puck control.

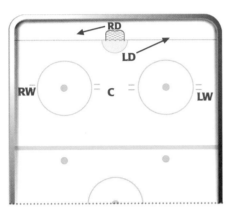

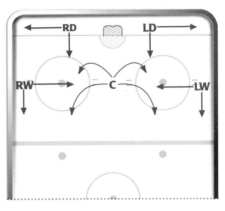

Each player has freedom to move about in the general area of his position. This allows the players to move for an initial outlet pass or to find an area that allows the offensive unit to control the puck.

A typical play has the defensemen pass the puck between themselves. The RD would pass to the RW, who in turn would pass to the Center. The LW would move up the ice. The RW can pass back to the RD to maintain puck control if they are not able to break out.

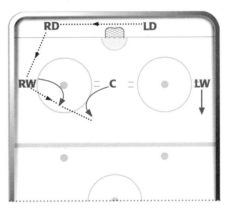

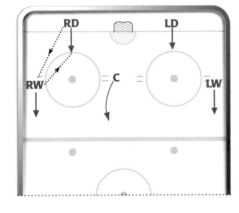

The RD moves up the ice and receives a return pass from the RW. The RD maintains control of the puck or passes to another forward.

NEUTRAL ZONE

The "puck-control" attack in the neutral zone is similar to the puck-control breakouts. The forwards are in the normal area of their position. The purpose of this type of attack in the neutral zone is to stay in control of the puck until the unit is positive it can move into the offensive zone.

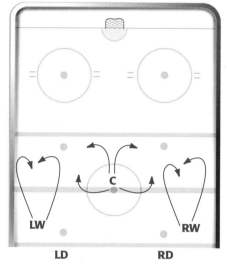

1 **Basic Alignment** The forwards are in their normal positions. The forwards have room to move in their areas. The defensemen are also in normal positions and are allowed to move around in their areas.

The forwards crisscross to **2** free one of them from a check or move to forward. In this example, the LW and Center move to their right, and the RW skates diagonally across the neutral zone.

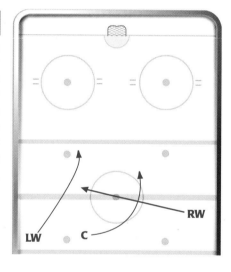

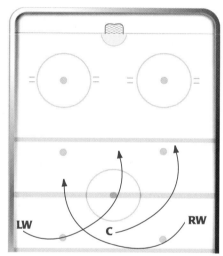

3 The RW swings deep toward the blue line in a diagonal arc across the neutral zone.

The defensemen **4** pass the puck between themselves. Meanwhile, the forwards move across the neutral zone (the LW and Center to the right, and the RW to the left). The LD can pass to any of the three forwards or can pass back to the RD.

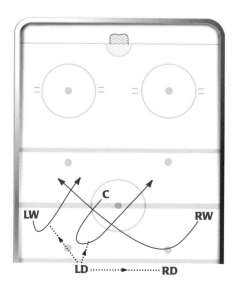

OFFENSIVE ZONE

The "triangular" offense is one method of executing a puck-control style of play in the offensive zone. The three forwards work in a triangular formation. This is done to create an opening for one forward. Passing, especially the "give-and-go," is important.

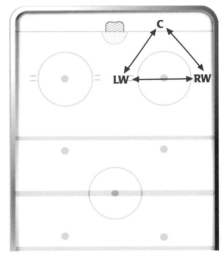

1 One possible triangle has one forward (C) deep along the boards, a second forward (RW) along the boards and the third forward (LW) in the slot. A second possible triangle has one forward (C) deep behind the goal and the other two forwards (LW and RW) wide in the face-off circles.

A third possible triangle has two forwards (LW and C) deep behind the goal line and the third forward (RW) in the slot. **2**

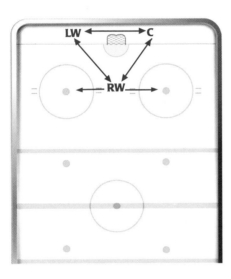

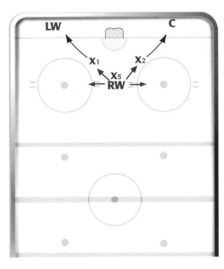

3 The triangle normally attempts to draw the opposition out of position. In this example, the LW and the Center attempt, through passes, to draw the defensemen (X1 and X2) away from the net. This will force a forward (X5) to cover both the net and the slot area.

This formation forces the opposition to play many situations man-to-man. If the offensive players are able to win one of the 1-on-1 situations, they will have a man who is open and moves to the net. In this example, the Center has beaten X2, creating a 2-on-1 situation, with X5 forced to cover both the RW and the Center. **4**

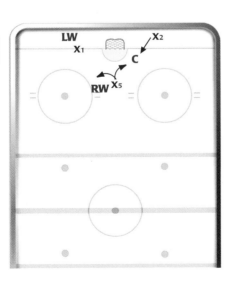

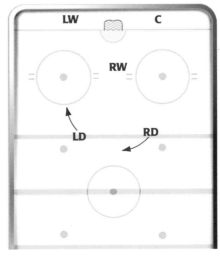

5 The defensemen are normally conservative and stay on the blue line. They are allowed to move to the high slot when the opportunity arises. When one defenseman (LD) moves in, the second defenseman (RD) moves back a few feet to cover.

Aggressive Play

KEY POINTS

Aggressive play is an advanced level of play designed to force the opposition into errors. Its purpose is to keep the offense on the initiative and to take away opportunities for the defensive initiative. Good basic skills, especially skating, are important, and it calls for good anticipation by the entire offensive unit. Seldom a starting point, this style of play is one that a team may advance to later in the season.

1. Aggressive play teaches the offense to exploit the opposition's weaknesses by attacking vulnerable positions, areas or players.

2. It encourages the offensive unit to be on the initiative at all times.

3. It helps the team develop anticipation.

4. It requires good skating and passing skills.

5. Teams need time to grow into successful aggressive-play strategies, but they should continue to strive for this level throughout the season.

BREAKOUTS

The "free-movement" breakout permits forwards to freewheel through their own end. While it may look as if there is no design to the play, the forwards are in fact setting specific plays in motion. Once a defenseman has gained control of the puck, the forwards begin to skate in preset patterns through their own end. The key to this breakout strategy is to have the forward constantly in motion to create confusion for the forecheckers and to position himself to receive a quick pass.

Play One. RD has the puck in the corner. The off-side wing (LW) moves across the slot toward center ice, forcing the opposition's defenseman off the blue line, while the RW moves across the slot toward the blue line and the Center swings toward the boards.

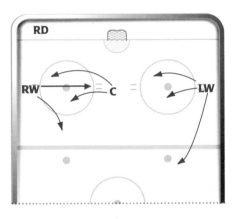

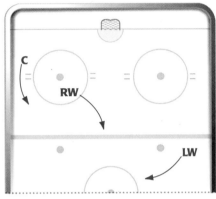

In one scenario, all three forwards skate toward the opposition's left side.

Play Two. The defenseman (RD) has the puck in the corner. The two wings (LW and RW) move down the ice off the boards toward the slot, while the Center either swings through the neutral zone or moves deep into the offensive zone.

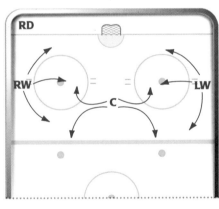

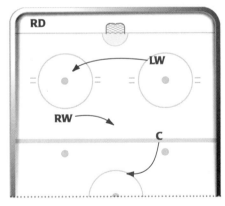

One result is that the moving Center forces the opposition's defensemen off the blue line, while the two wings crisscross in the defensive zone.

Play Three. The defenseman (RD) has the puck in the corner. The puck-side wing (RW) moves to the neutral zone, forcing the opposition's defenseman off the blue line. The Center swings toward the puck while the off-side wing (LW) moves off the boards toward the slot.

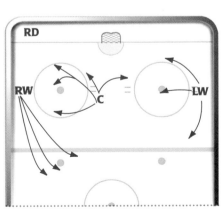

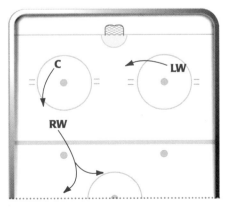

This play lets one wing (RW) move directly to the neutral zone, thereby forcing the defenseman to vacate the blue line and allowing the Center and the other wing (LW) to skate in that direction.

NEUTRAL ZONE

The "free-movement" neutral-zone play is similar to the breakout plays. What may appear to be free skating are really predesigned plays. The objective of the neutral-zone play is to move quickly to the offense and attack the opposition's blue-line area.

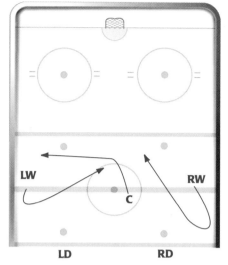

1 One possible play: The LD has the puck near the blue line, the two wings cut toward the middle of the ice, and the Center moves up to and along the blue line.

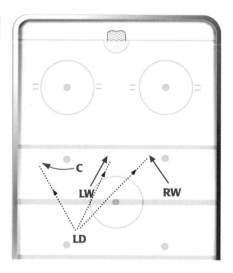

2 All three forwards are in a position to receive a pass and move to the offensive zone. The Center may have forced the opposition's RD to move back into his defensive zone or across the ice. This would free the area that the LW and RW are skating toward.

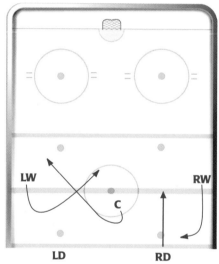

3 A second possible play: The LD has the puck near the blue line, and the LW and the Center crisscross, moving toward the blue line. The RW swings back toward the blue line, and the RD moves quickly up the ice.

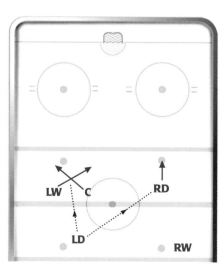

4 The result has the RD, the Center and the LW in position to receive a pass and move to the offensive zone. The crisscrossing by the LW and the Center forces the opposition's RD to cover both men.

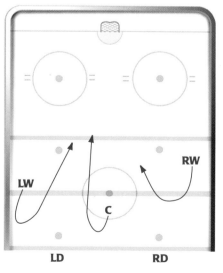

5 A third possible play has all three forwards moving toward the offensive zone in the middle of the neutral zone. The LD has the puck. The result is that the three forwards flood or overload the middle of the neutral zone. This allows the LD to pass to any of the three and have the forwards quickly on the attack.

OFFENSIVE ZONE

Aggressive play in the offensive zone attacks the net and slot area. This is usually done by overloading the slot, which makes it difficult for the opposition to defend the net and slot area. Aggressive play puts constant pressure on the net and slot area.

The forwards **1** go to the net and slot when a defenseman (LD) has the puck.

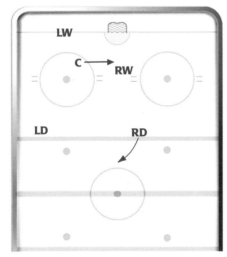

2 The forwards place themselves in position for tip-ins, deflections and rebounds. They also make it difficult for the opposition's defenseman to control the net and slot area.

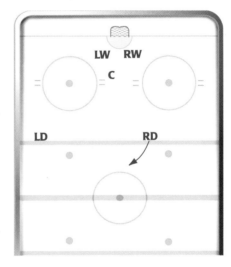

The normal **3** positioning has one forward (RW) in the slot, a second forward (LW) deep in the zone and the third forward (C) in a position where he can move to the slot or deep into the zone.

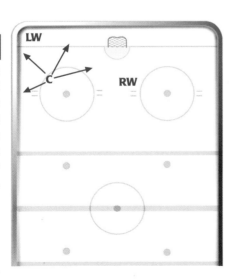

4 The initial attempt to make the play on the net has the Center go to the net. This will force a defenseman (X2) to cover both the Center and the RW if the other defenseman (X1) is on the puck in the corner and the forward (X5) does not cover in front.

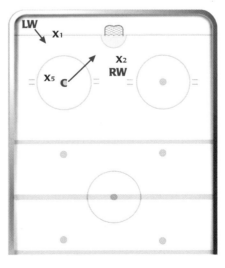

TACTICAL DRYLAND PRACTICE

*"To strive, to seek, to find, and
not to yield."*

Alfred, Lord Tennyson
"Ulysses"

CHAPTER FIVE

THE ECONOMICS OF TEACHING TACTICS ENCOURAGES THE USE OF DRYLAND PRACTICES. THE cost of ice time, as well as its limited availability, forces coaches to make their practices efficient. Three general areas—conditioning, skills and tactics—need to be covered. Dryland sessions provide additional practice time that is especially beneficial for teaching tactics.

The coach can utilize tactical dryland practices to teach knowledge of the system, an understanding of positional responsibility, movement of the unit, recognition of the different situations and the options for offensive and defensive units, and the flow of play.

The type of facility needed for dryland sessions is flexible. A ballfield, parking lot, gym floor, even a rink with no ice can suffice. If the practice surface is close to regulation size of one zone, then tactics used in the three zones can be adequately taught.

My suggestion is not to use sticks while covering tactics. It is better to toss a volleyball or a team handball. The idea is to educate the players on the system. Walking through the different steps while tossing the ball is sufficient instruction. The execution of any system can be practiced during on-ice sessions.

This chapter illustrates a step-by-step method for teaching systems on dryland. The steps are explanation, movement of play, recognition of situations, flow of play and on-ice execution. Two systems will be used as examples: "wings play the off-side" power play and a "positional breakout."

WINGS PLAY THE OFF-SIDE POWER PLAY

This power play has the wings playing their off-side, spread wide apart. The Center plays close to the net. The wings are the primary shooters, with the defensemen the secondary shooters. The Center is the key playmaker as well as the primary screen man and rebounder.

1A **Explanation.** The team with a man advantage should make maximum use of the power play. The power play lasts for 2 minutes, so there is no reason to hurry the play. If an opponent can be eliminated, then the man advantage becomes a two-man advantage. This can be done either by trapping the player in the offensive zone or getting him to play out of position.

1B Stress the proper positional alignment in the offensive zone. Each player must know his position and that of the other players. This makes the power play more effective, since the players are able to interchange positions.

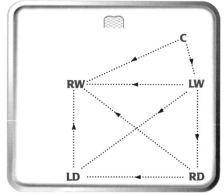

1C The key to this power play is the flow of the puck. The players can remain stationary, pass the puck around and force the opposition to commit themselves, which will create the scoring opportunities.

1D The primary shooter should be the off-side wing (RW). However, if the opposition checks the off-side wing too closely, there is room for the off-side defenseman (LD) to move into the slot.

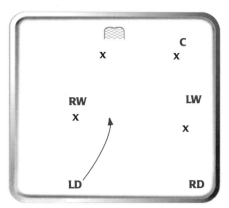

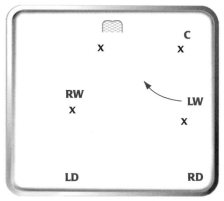

1E Also, the on-side (LW) has access to the slot, particularly if the opposition forwards check the points too closely.

1F Each player should be aware of the different zone responsibilities.This knowledge is essential— it emphasizes the proper positional alignments and prevents two or three players from bunching up. With a man advantage, this power play should use as much ice as possible.

2_A **Movement of Play.**
Movement means five men moving. Everyone is aware of the movements of the other players. This will prevent a pass from going to a spot that has been evacuated by a player. Giveaways such as this should never occur on the power play.

Movement should be **2**_B 1) in accordance with the movement of the puck and 2) in accordance with an anticipated play.

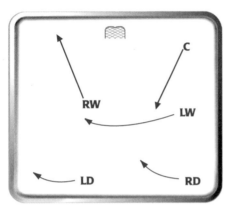

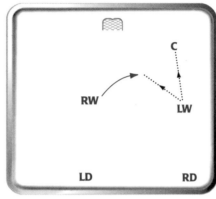

2_C When a player all of a sudden is alone in a scoring position and the puck comes to him, it reflects anticipation by at least two players—the shooter and the passer.

Illustrate how the **2**_D power play fails if one player does not execute properly. The left wing (LW), for example, gets out of position.

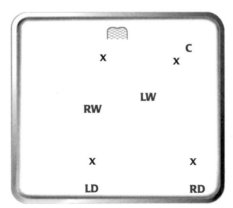

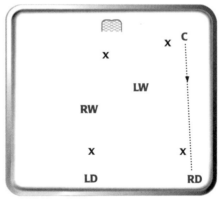

2_E When the LW is out of position, it prevents the Center (C) from passing to the point, since the left wing is normally a relay.

The Center is **2**_F forced instead to pass through the opposition or walk the pass out.

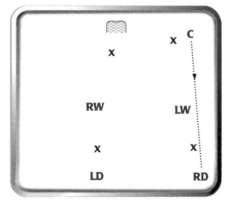

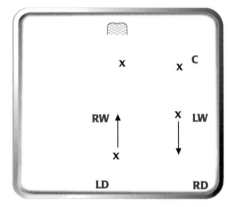

3ₐ **Recognition of Situations.** Review the different penalty-killing systems: standard box, tight box, man in slot, etc. This is much easier if preparing for a specific team that uses only one style. (Diagram 3A-3C)

3ʙ This is a standard box system. The wings normally cover the points. They can also collapse to pressure the two opposing wings.

The wing covering the LD has moved **3ᴄ** to the RW to prevent him from receiving a pass and shooting.

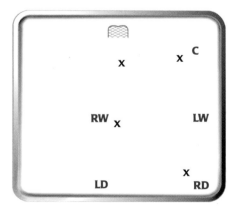

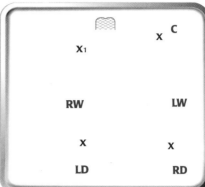

3ᴅ Work on what the five-man unit does when an opponent gets out of position, creating a scoring opportunity. For example, the defenseman (X1) gets too far to the wrong side of the net.

This **3ᴇ** permits the RW to move into the low slot.

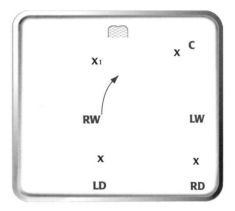

3ꜰ It also permits the LW to move into the slot. Walk through these situations so that everyone is aware of the possibilities.

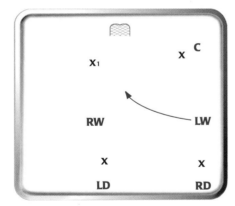

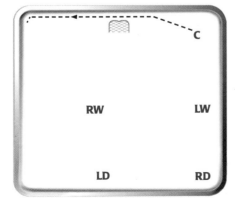

3ɢ Work on interchanging the players in reaction to different situations. For example, the Center shoots the puck along the boards.

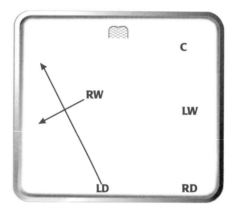

3ₕ The LD is able to reach the puck fastest, so he sets up in the corner and the RW takes his normal position.

The RD covers for the LD, the LW covers for the RD, and the Center covers for the LW. **3ᵢ**

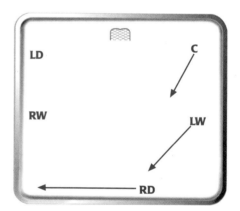

3ⱼ This is the proper alignment.

Flow of Play. **4**_A Have the players toss a volleyball around the system formation. This allows them to be aware of their teammates' movements and their tendencies to move in certain directions.

4_B Practice the flow of play in three progressive steps:
1) With no opposition;
2) With chairs or pylons set up to simulate the opposition;
3) With actual players as the penalty killers.

4_C The tempo of the session will depend on the skills of the players. Begin at a slow walking pace, and increase the tempo as the players develop both their skills and their knowledge of the system.

On-Ice Execution. **5** During the on-ice practice, the time for strategy can be spent on the execution of the system. The groundwork should already have been covered during the dryland sessions. The ice time can be better spent in the actual perfection of the power play.

POSITIONAL BREAKOUT

This breakout has the three forwards in basic positions. One defenseman is behind the net, and the other is in front of the net.

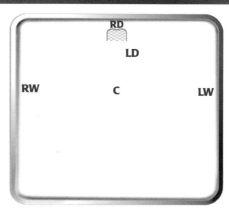

1A **Explanation.** Emphasize the proper positional alignment. Each player must know his position and that of his teammates.

1B The key to the breakout is the defenseman's short and quick outlet pass. It is critical that each player play his position.

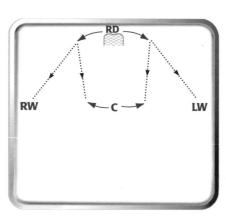

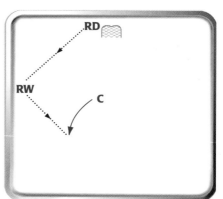

1C This breakout normally has two passes to clear the zone. For example, the RD passes to the RW, who, in turn, passes to the Center.

1D Cover each possible situation. This includes options for both forward and defensemen. For example, the LD can move to the corner for an outlet pass from the RD.

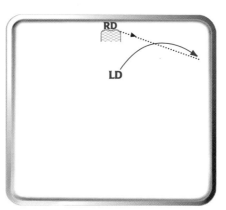

2A **Movement of Play.** Movement means five men moving. Everyone is aware of the possible movements of the other players.

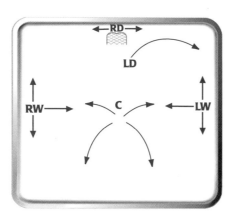

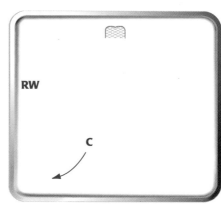

2B Movement should be in accordance with: (1) the movement of the puck and (2) an anticipated play. One player moving on his own can ruin a play—if the Center moves ahead of the play the wings have no one to make the second outlet pass to.

Recognition of Situations.
Review what the opposition players may do to stop the breakout. For example, they may put their wings on the wings and the Center in the middle to prevent a pass to a forward.

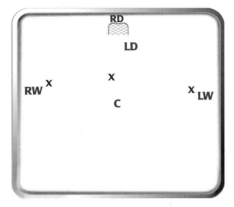

Work on how the unit should react to the opposition. For example, the LD moves to one corner, and the Center to the other corner. This puts two players deep in the zone, and the RD should be able to pass to one.

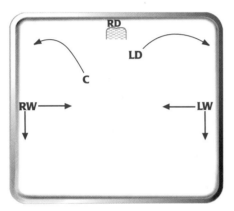

Flow of Play. Have the players toss a volleyball while going through the steps of the breakout play. This allows the players to be aware of the possible movements and to become familiar with the unit's movements.

Practice the flow of play in three progressive steps:
(1) With no opposition;
(2) With chairs or pylons set up to simulate the opposition;
(3) With actual players as the opposition.

The tempo of the session will depend on the skills and knowledge of the players. Begin at a slow walking pace, and gradually increase the tempo as the players develop both their skills and knowledge of the system.

On-Ice Execution. During the on-ice practice, the time for tactics should be spent on the actual execution of the system. The groundwork should have been covered during the off-ice session. The ice time can be better spent in the actual perfection of the breakout play.

PLANNING & ORGANIZATION FOR THE SEASON

"The selection of a site for a new farm was always based, in part, on the availability of a good supply of clean, cold water. "I've got a good, bold spring" is a sentence we have heard hundreds of times, and it is always said with pride and satisfaction."

Foxfire 4

CHAPTER SIX

A PREREQUISITE TO EVERY ASPECT OF COACHING IS PROPER PLANNING. Team success, which usually reflects coaching success, is dependent on the use of organizational skills. Poor organizational skills hinder the coaching process as well as the development of the team. Sound coaching techniques begin with planning and organization.

There are three kinds of questions every coach must consider when he sits down to make his plan for the season. The first concerns the different elements of coaching, such as the team roster, game schedules and the practice calendar, which must include time for conditioning, skills training and tactical and systems training. How are the elements related? Is there a priority for the elements? Is the coach especially strong in one area? Do the priorities change during the season? As a coach, you'll have to give serious thought to these needs through good sound planning.

The second set of questions focuses on the team. What is the level of competition? How successful was the team last year? What are the team's strengths and weaknesses? What are the team's goals for this year? What style of play will the team use? Which systems will be utilized? Which drills will be needed to complement the style of play and systems? The questions again are numerous but must be considered when implementing a season's plan.

The final questions concern the individual players on the team. What is the skill level of the players? What are the strengths and weaknesses of the individual players? What skills are needed for the planned style of play and systems? Does the team have good leaders among its players? From which players do you anticipate problems? What can be done to prevent or alleviate them? Proper time and attention should be given to dealing with the individual players, both as a group and individually. A season's plan needs to provide the essential time to attend to the individual players.

This chapter will provide an example of a season-long coaching plan. It will include goals for the seasons, types of practices to be used, tactical plans for the team, a season-long conditioning plan, time for coach-player meetings and provisions to alter the plan if the team is not meeting anticipated levels.

Everything the coach does during the season is based on the season's plan. A good plan helps to eliminate or control the problems that inevitably arise. The plan serves as a reference point during the season. This is particularly useful when things are not going well. A plan that has been implemented with proper thought and detail prevents impromptu changes. It is precisely the constant occurrence of these problems and situations that warrants a plan.

DESCRIPTION OF TEAM: The team has an 18-player roster in a league comprising 15- and 16-year-old players. It is anticipated that 12 to 14 players will be 16 years old, with the remainder being 15. Between 10 and 12 players will have played last year. Last year's record was 14-17-5, with a play-off record of 1-2-0. The league has nine other teams. Each team plays every other team four times during the season, twice at home and twice away. The longest trip is approximately 75 minutes by car. The schedule calls for two games a week, on Wednesdays and Saturdays. Normally, there will be one home and one away game each week. The team has practice time twice a week: on Mondays and Fridays for 60 minutes. The team has two coaches, who are both back for a second year.

League rules permit two weeks of four practices each prior to the start of the season. The league mandates that each team must have two weeks of off-ice training prior to the start of on-ice practices.

Six teams make the play-offs. The top two finishing clubs receive byes in the first round. Each round consists of a best-of-three schedule. The championship round is the best of five.

A general preview of the players indicates that the players' ability level will not be significantly different from last year. There are not likely to be any

dominating players, although there will be a consistent level of skill throughout the club. The skill level is adequate. With 10 to 12 players returning, the team will be more experienced than last year's. The team is not especially quick but has enough size to compensate for what it lacks in overall team quickness. The goaltending should be strong, with a returning 16-year-old whose record last year was 9-8-1. The second goalie will be one of two 15-year-olds whose records were 17-3-5 and 11-5-4 on last year's team of 14-year-olds.

The coaches' strengths are in skill development and conditioning. Their tactical approach will lean toward conservative, stressing strong positional play. They are not confident or comfortable playing an aggressive, wide-open style of hockey. They anticipate introducing a second system of forechecking and power play by midseason. The team's strength, however, will be mastering the systems used by last year's team. The major priority for the coaches is to develop the individual skills and the team concept. A .500 season in a competitive league would be considered an excellent year.

The Plan

Goals

1. Improvement in skills area.

2. Improvement in the team concept.

3. Maintain a high level of conditioning.

4. A .500 season.

1. Practices will include tactical, conditioning and skill drills.

2. Every practice will end with a fun competitive drill.

3. The team will begin the season with a 1-2-2 forechecking system and comparable systems for the other zones.

4. The team will use three types of practices during the season.

Practices

Season: 75 minutes

Type 1 (PS1)
30% skills
30% tactical
25% conditioning
15% fun competition

Type 2 (PS2)
40% tactical
25% skills
25% conditioning
10% fun competition

Season: 60 minutes

Type 1 (P1)
50% tactical
20% skills
20% conditioning
10% fun competition

Type 2 (P2)
50% skills
20% tactical
20% conditioning
10% fun competition

Type 3 (P3)
30% skills
30% tactical
30% conditioning
10% fun competition

Season Calendar

Week	Monday	Wednesday	Friday	Saturday
1 (pre-season)	PS2	PS1	PS1	PS2
2 (pre-season)	PS2	PS1	PS2	PS1
3	P1	G	P3	G
4	P2	G	P1	G
5	P1	G	P2	G
6	P2	G	P3	G
7	P1	G	P2	G
8	P2	G	P3	G
9	P1	G	P2	G
10	P1	G	P3	G
11	P3	G	P1	G
12	P1	G	P2	G
13	P2	G	P3	G
14	P1	G	P2	G
15	P3	G	P2	G
16	P3	G	P3	G
17	P2	G	P1	G
18	P2	G	P1	G
19	P1	G	P2	G
20	P2	G	P3	G

Notes:

—Much of the tactical time will be spent on drills that emphasize team play, such as breakouts, power plays, forechecking, neutral-zone counterattacks, etc.

—Every practice will end with a competition-type drill, such as show-downs, relay races, etc.

—Emphasis will be on the team developing puck-control skills.

—Time tests will periodically be used to evaluate improvements in quickness, agility, passing and puckhandling.

—Players will be given a calisthenics program to do on their own at home.

—Some new systems will be introduced near the midseason mark. For weeks 8, 9 and 10, practices will place more time and emphasis on tactics.

—Coaches will meet with individual players during weeks 3 and 4, 11 and 12, and 17 and 18.

Tactics

NOTES

Start of the year:

Forechecking—Basic 1-2-2

Defensive Zone—Zone coverage

Breakouts—Balanced positional play

Neutral Zone—1-2-2 defensively,

positional play offensively

Power Play—Funnel with three

forwards in the slot area

Penalty Killing—Basic 1-1-2

Midseason:

Forechecking—1-1-3 encouraging

some aggressive play

Power Play—2-1-2

Penalty Killing—2-2

1. Early in the year, place emphasis on learning the positional approach to the team play.

2. Drills for passing, puckhandling and shooting will mirror team's systems as often as possible.

3. If team masters the systems introduced early in the year, a few new systems, which encourage aggressiveness with positional play, will be introduced.

4. Early in the year, all the players will practice the special situations (power play and man down) and play in the games. A decision about using special teams will be made at midseason.

Off-Ice Training.

Four different workouts
for the two-week period.

1 Mondays:
Warm-ups (15 min.)
Interval running (35 min.)
Run 60 sec./rest 180 sec. 4 times
Run 20 sec./rest 80 sec. 6 times
Run 6 sec./rest 24 sec. 6 times
Hockey-skill circuit (30 min.)
Warm-down (5 min.)

2 Wednesdays:
Warm-ups (15 min.)
Aerobic run (15 min.)
1¼ to 2 miles
Volleyball (15 min.)
Three teams of six each, rotate
teams every three points
Calisthenics (10 min.)
Hockey-skill circuit (15 min.)
Warm-down (5 min.)

3 Fridays:
Warm-ups (15 min.)
Aerobic run (15 min.)
1¼ to 2 miles
Soccer game (20 min.)
Three teams of six each, rotate
after every goal
Breakout plays (15 min.)
Players go through team's different
breakouts using volleyball.
Hockey-skill circuit (15 min.)
Warm-down (5 min.)

4 Saturdays:
Warm-ups (15 min.)
Volleyball (20 min.)
Three teams of six each, rotate
teams every three points
Football (20 min.)
Three teams of six each, rotate
every four downs, each team has
four downs to go 25 yards to score.
Warm-down (5 min.)

Goalies.
5
Every practice will have goalie-
oriented shooting drills.
An off-ice practice consisting of agility,
mobility and skill drills will be given to
the goalies to do at home.
The goalies will be warmed up off-ice
prior to each practice.
The goalies will know in advance when
they are playing the games.

EXAMPLE PRACTICE 1

TYPE 1 (P1)

0-5
Warm-Ups. **1**
Light skating, doing turns, spins, falls, etc., with and without pucks.

6-15
Three Skill Drills. **2ᴀ**
Three drills, one in each zone: Backward skating on a face-off circle.

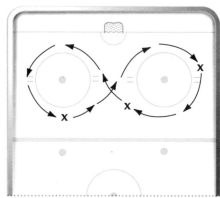

2ʙ Players skate figure-8s while stickhandling.

Players make passes while standing still on a face-off circle. **2ᴄ**

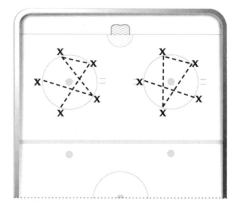

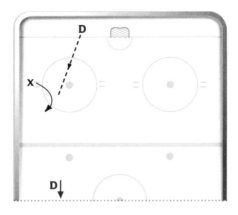

3A **16-30**
Breakout Drills.
Defenseman begins
1-on-1 drill with an
outlet pass.

Defenseman
begins 2-on-1 **3B**
drill with an outlet pass.

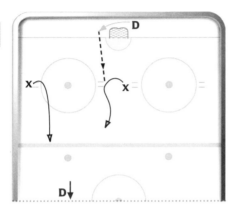

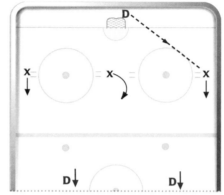

3C Defenseman
begins 3-on-1
and 3-on-2 drills with
an outlet pass.

31-35 **4**
Conditioning Drill.
Players skate 1½ laps,
skate 22 seconds, rest 44
seconds. Three times.

36-40 **5**
Passing Drill.
Pairs make one-touch
pass while moving in
one zone. Six players
in each zone.

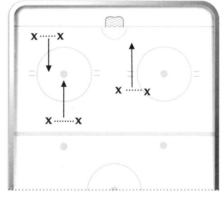

41-50 **6**
Forechecking.
Instruction on
forechecking system.
Players go through
system and possible
adjustments of the
opposition.

51-55 **7**
Conditioning Drill.
Players skate hard to the
blue line, turn and come
back to the goal line
easy. Skate 4 seconds
and rest 12 seconds. Six
to eight times.

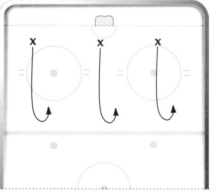

8 **56-60**
Relay Race.
Teams of four players
each skate down and
back once.

EXAMPLE PRACTICE 2

TYPE 1 (P1)

0-5
Warm-Ups. **1**
Skating easy,
players in groups of
three pass the puck
between themselves.
One player skates back-
ward, two forward.

6-15 Two
Shooting Drills. **2ᴀ**
One in each end. Player
breaks off wing and
shoots.

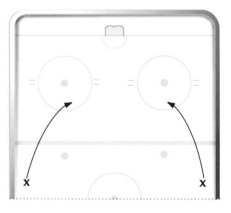

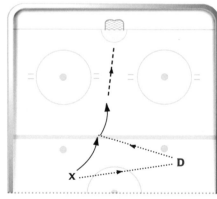

2ᴮ Forward passes
to defenseman,
breaks to the net,
receives a return pass
and shoots.

16-22
Defensive - **3**
Zone Coverage.
Instruction on
defensive-zone
coverage.

4 **23-28**
Counterattack.
Three forwards begin
3-on-2 attack with
outlet pass from a
defenseman. Drill goes
both ways.

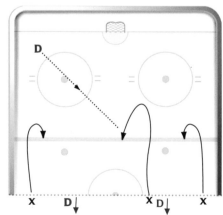

TYPE 1 (P1)

29-35
Conditioning Drill.
Players skate down and
back. Skate 15 seconds
and rest 45 seconds.
Five times.

36-40
Stickhandling Drill.
Players skate laps and
weave around pylons.

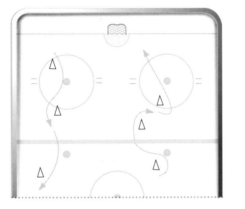

Players skate
laps and make
circles around pylons.

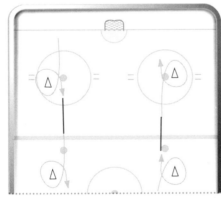

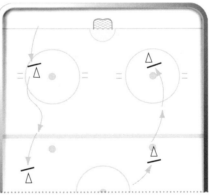

Players skate
laps and stop
at pylons.

41-55
Power Play
and Penalty Killing.
Instruction and
execution of power-
play and man-down
situations.

56-60
Target Shooting.
From the blue line, play-
ers try to hit Frisbee that
is hanging from the net.

EXAMPLE PRACTICE 3

TYPE 2 (P2)

1 **0-5**
Warm-Ups.
Players skate easy in pairs and pass the puck between themselves and then play 1-on-1. Executed while skating laps.

6-10
Shooting Drill. **2**
Players swing out of the corners and shoot on the goal. Use both ends of the rink.

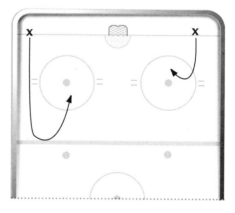

11-20
Passing Drills. **3ᴀ**
Two drills executed on face-off circle. Stationary passing on face-off circle.

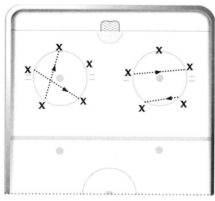

3ʙ Make pass to man ahead while skating around face-off circle.

21-27 **4**
Neutral-Zone
Counterattack.
Instruction on
the neutral-zone
counterattack.

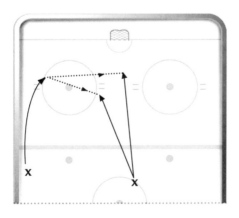

5 **28-35**
Conditioning Drill.
Skate width of the ice,
over and back. Skate 12
seconds and rest 36
seconds. Six times.

36-43 **6**
Puckhandling Drill.
Players work on taking a
pass in the feet and
deflecting the puck to
the stick.

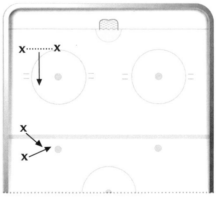

7 **44-50**
Stickhandling
Drill.
Players working in pairs
begin passing the puck
between themselves.
On whistle, they play
1-on-1, trying to keep
the puck to themselves.

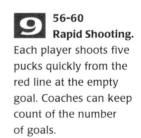

8 **51-55**
Shooting Drill.
One player moves to the
corner with a puck.
Second player moves to
the slot area and shoots
or deflects pass from the
first player.

9 **56-60**
Rapid Shooting.
Each player shoots five
pucks quickly from the
red line at the empty
goal. Coaches can keep
count of the number
of goals.

EXAMPLE PRACTICE 4

TYPE 2 (P2)

0-5
Warm-Ups. **1**
Start with light, easy
skating, and gradually
pick up the tempo.

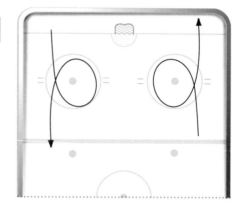

2 **6-10**
Stickhandling D
Players, in groups of fo
or five, skate circles at
each face-off circle whi
carrying the puck.

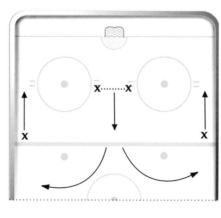

3ᴀ **11-25**
Skill Drills.
Player moves with the puck
from the corner toward the
net or the slot area to shoot.

Two players **3**ʙ
skate up-ice
making short passes
and come back wide,
each carrying the puck.

3ᴄ The players
each have a
puck and try to avoid
each other while movin
in the neutral zone.

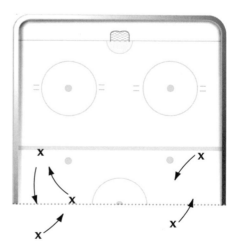

26-30
Face-Offs. **4**
Instructions
on face-offs.

31-40
Conditioning Drill. **5**
In groups of four or five
players, skate two laps.
Skate 30 seconds and
rest 90 seconds.
Four times.

6 **41-50**
Power Play and
Penalty Killing.
Using units, practice
both the power-play and
man-down situations.

51-60
Games of 3 vs. 3 **7**
Using the width of the
ice, play three separate
games of 3 vs. 3.
Emphasize quick,
short passes.

EXAMPLE PRACTICE 5

TYPE 3 (P3)

0-5
Warm-Ups. **1**
Easy skating and stretching. Skate three laps, each at a quicker tempo.

6-15
Skating Drills. **2**ₐ
Two drills. Players skate to the blue line, stop, then take two or three quick strides in the other direction.

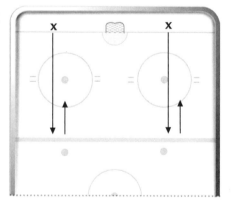

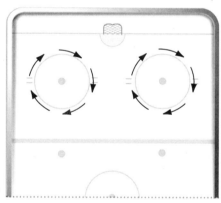

2ᵦ Work on forward and backward crossovers while skating on a face-off circle.

16-25
Aerobic Skate. **3**
Players skate at 60% to 70% maximum speed continuously in laps. Skate 3 minutes and rest 1 minute. Two times.

4 **26-40**
Forechecking and Breakouts.
Working with two units in each end, practice forechecking systems and breakout plays.

41-50
Skill Drills. 5A
Three drills.
Players work on
taking pass off
the boards.

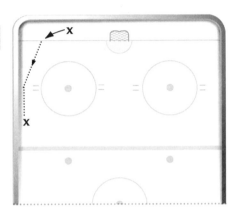

5B Players work
on turns by
skating figure-8s, going
hard on turns and easy
on straightaways.

Shooting drill
has player 5C
receive a pass as he
moves into slot area
and shoots.

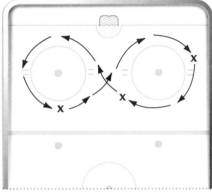

51-55 6
Conditioning Drill.
Players work short, quick
intervals by skating hard
for 5 seconds and rest
20 seconds while
carrying a puck.
Eight times.

7 **56-60**
Showdown.

EXAMPLE PRACTICE 6

TYPE 3 (P3)

0-5
Warm-Ups.
Easy skating, with players working in pairs shadowing each other.

2 **6-10**
Shooting Drill.
Players come off boards and shoot.

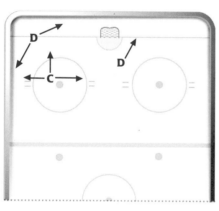

11-20
Checking.
Centers and defensemen work on coverage in the net and the slot area.

3A

3B Wings work on covering checks while backchecking.

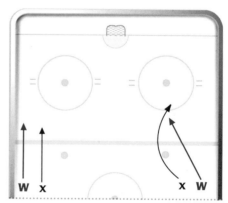

21-35
Conditioning Drill.
Players skate three laps. Skate 60 seconds and rest 180 seconds. Three times.

36-45
Skating Drills.
Two skating drills.
Players work on
stepovers.

gility training,
with players
moving in all four
directions.

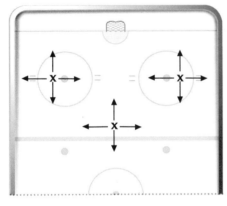

46-50
Breakout Play.
Units break out 5-on-2
to neutral zone, regroup,
then break out a second
time. Work both ends.

51-55
Conditioning Drill.
Players skate between
goal line and blue line
continuously.
Skate 15 seconds and
rest 45 seconds.
Four times.

56-60
Agility Test.
Players are timed while
skating an agility course.
(Approximately 20
seconds.)

MICHAEL A. SMITH

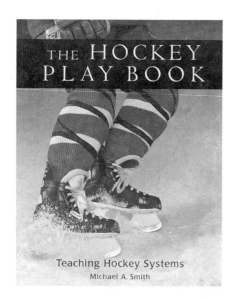

THE HOCKEY PLAY BOOK

Teaching Hockey Systems
224 pages. Black-and-white illustrations throughout. 8½" x 11"
Softcover. $22.95

In *The Hockey Play Book*, Mike Smith presents a straight-forward strategy for teaching hockey systems, first outlining each system's underlying philosophy and then providing an analytical breakdown of each system that is accompanied by illustrated drills and step-by-step methods. A longtime coach, adviser and friend of the sport, Smith has created an invaluable guide that can be adapted and adjusted by coaches to capitalize on the strengths of the team.

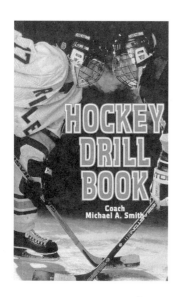

THE HOCKEY DRILL BOOK

224 pages. Black-and-white illustrations throughout. 4¼" x 7"
Softcover. $12.95

No player or team is too good to skip regular practice sessions. For young players and inexperienced teams, practice is the only way to improve basic skills and to learn the fundamentals. Mike Smith's *The Hockey Drill Book* will provide coaches everywhere with an accessible source of new, reliable practice drills. Smith's handbook covers the fundamentals of skating, stickhandling, passing, shooting, conditioning, goaltending, checking and game situations and includes drills complete with diagrams, descriptions and recommended variations.

Published by Firefly Books